READING
VERSUS
THE REST

1920 ~ 2007

By Dave Twydell

Published by:
Yore Publications
12 The Furrows, Harefield,
Middx. UB9 6AT.

British Library Cataloguing-in-Publication Data.
A catalogue record for this book
is available from the British Library.

ISBN 978 0 9552949 7 6

Printed and bound by:
The Cromwell Press, Trowbridge

Introduction

This book records memorable events that relate to every club that Reading F.C. have met in Senior competitions since 1920, that event being a match or matches, notable players, or other situations. Each feature does not necessarily relate to the best game, the biggest victory (or defeat) etc., but attempts to highlight the interesting and the unusual in Reading's long history; an historical book tackled in an entirely different way.

Such an historical book, compiled and written about Reading Football Club but not by a supporter, is normally not the ideal credentials. But as the Publisher of two former best selling Reading books - 'Royals Remembered' (Players' Who's Who) and 'Heaven On Earth' (History) I had much of the material at my fingertips. In addition my own specific interest in the historical side of the game, non-League football and the former League clubs adds to my 'qualifications' for the task. Finally, and particularly relevant, I actually lived for nearly two years, in the mid 1960's, in one of the roads literally a long goal kick away from the old Elm Park Ground.

The writing, the compilation of the facts, the statistics and the sourcing of the illustrations would not have been possible without the enthusiastic help of two Reading F.C. experts, David Downs and Alan Sedunary (the latter the author of the two aforementioned books), plus Tony Brown of SoccerData. There are several excellent independent web sites on the club, in particular 'www.royals.org' and associate links, from where a number of facts were gleaned or confirmed.

Dave Twydell
September 2007

Notes:

Opposition clubs and the statistical records consist of those played only in the Football League (all four divisions), F.A.Cup and Football League Cup matches - all under various titles. The statistical records do not include play-off matches, but when # is added this acknowldeges that such additional matches have been played. Where F.A.Cup matches have extended to extra time the final score after this extra period has been included in the goals record. When matches have resulted in a penalty shoot-out (after extra time has been played), this has been noted >, but penalty goals have not been included. Where matches have been played on a Neutral ground, in the statistics these have been considered as an 'away' fixture in the record, and noted $.

Only matches from the 1920/21 season (Reading's entry into the Football League) have been considered. However, in respect of F.A.Cup matches prior to 1920, although these records have not been included in the statistics, such additional matches are noted * to indicate such additions. A number of additional clubs have also been encountered, pre-1920, in the F.A.Cup and F.A.Amateur Cup, and although these clubs have not been featured, a list of them has been separately included. Names: With respect to current Football League clubs their current name is given, despite possibly having an earlier name when the feature versus Reading occurred. In respect of non-League clubs, their name at the time of the Reading feature is given.

Copyright:
Grateful thanks to David Downs for his help in tracing many of the illustrations. In the majority of cases, the source of the photographs and illustrations used are not identified on the actual item (and whilst not specifically identified as such, no doubt some have originated from The Reading Evening Post and The Reading Chronicle), therefore apologies are offered by the Publisher and Author, should copyright have inadvertently been breached. However, acknowledgements are given to the following known sources (as stated on the photograph) but who have not been traced: Middleton, Lincoln; Collier, Reading; Bob Thomas, Northampton; Goodall (Rotherham photograph), and Steve Peters.

Clubs played in competitive matches: 1920/21 - 2006/07

Football League
(Present and Past)

Aberdare Athletic
Accrington Stanley
Aldershot
Arsenal
Aston Villa
Barnet
Barnsley
Barrow
Birmingham City
Blackburn Rovers
Blackpool
Bolton Wanderers
Bournemouth (AFC)
Bradford City
Bradford (Park Avenue)
Brentford
Brighton & Hove Albion
Bristol City
Bristol Rovers
Burnley
Bury
Cambridge United
Cardiff City
Carlisle United
Charlton Athletic
Chelsea
Chester City
Chesterfield
Colchester United
Coventry City
Crewe Alexandra

Crystal Palace
Darlington
Derby County
Doncaster Rovers
Everton
Exeter City
Fulham
Gillingham
Grimsby Town
Halifax Town
Hartlepool United
Hereford United
Huddersfield Town
Hull City
Ipswich Town
Leeds United
Leicester City
Leyton Orient
Lincoln City
Liverpool
Luton Town
Macclesfield Town
Manchester City
Manchester United
Mansfield Town
Merthyr Town (& Tydfil)
Middlesbrough
Millwall
Newcastle United
Newport County
Northampton Town

Norwich City
Nottingham Forest
Notts. County
Oldham Athletic
Oxford United
Peterborough United
Plymouth Argyle
Port Vale
Portsmouth
Preston North End
Queen's Park Rangers
Rochdale
Rotherham United
Scunthorpe United
Sheffield United
Sheffield Wednesday
Shrewsbury Town
South Shields
Southampton
Southend United
Southport

Stockport County
Stoke City
Sunderland
Swansea City
Swindon Town
Thames Association
Torquay United
Tottenham Hotspur
Tranmere Rovers
Walsall
Watford
West Bromwich Albion
West Ham United
Wigan Athletic
Wimbledon
Wolverhampton Wanderers
Workington
Wrexham
Wycombe Wanderers
York City
(103 Total)

FA Cup only:

Barking
Barry Town
Bedford Town
Bishop Stortford
Blyth Spartans
Bognor Regis Town
Brentwood Town
Bridgwater Town
Bromley
Cheltenham Town
Corinthians
Dagenham
Dartford
Enfield
Erith & Belvedere
Grays Athletic

Guildford City
Hayes
Hendon
Ilford
Kettering Town
Kings Lynn
Leyton
Maidstone United
Slough Town
Sutton Town
Wealdstone
Welling United
Weymouth
Wisbech Town
Yeovil Town
(31 Total)

League Cup only:
Boston United

(Overall Total 135 Different clubs)

Notes:

One 'combined' club is included - Merthyr Town/Tydfil (played in League and - as a reformed non-League club - in the F.A.Cup).

League Cup - Reading were drawn to play Maidstone United (1992/93 season), but the Kent club folded just before the start of the season. However this club is amongst Reading's competitors since they played them previously (as a non-League club) in the F.A.Cup.

In the F.A.Cup Welling United have been played the most times (five games), but only two separate ties (the rest were replays).

The period covered is from Reading's entry to the Football League in 1920. Other matches were played with other clubs in the F.A.Cup (from 1877) and the F.A.Amateur Cup (1893/4 - 1894/5).

The following additional clubs were played pre-1920:
F.A.Cup from 1877 and F.A.Amateur cup from 1893/94 to 1894/95 (One game per club except where number of games shown in brackets. A = Amateur Cup)

Bedminster
Bristol St.George (2)
Castleford Town
Casuals (A)
Chesham Town
Chesham (A)
Chesham Generals
Chesham Generals (A)
Clifton Association (3)
Dulwich
Eastleigh LSRW
Gainsborough Trinity
Hendon (1st club) (2)
Hotspur
Maidenhead (3, A)
Marlow
Newbury (2)
Old Westminsters (A)

Old St. Pauls
Old Etonians
Old Carthusians (1) + (1A)
Oxford City
Richmond Association
Rochester (2)
Royal Ordnance Factories (A)
Royal Engineers
South Reading (2)
South Bank (A)
South Norwood
Southall
Swifts
Upton Park (3)
Uxbridge
Warmley (3)
West End
(35 total)

From Aberdare to York,
and Plymouth to Newcastle
each end of the alphabet
and the geographical extremes.
****

From the Third Division...
...Third Division (South)...
...Second Division...
Third Division (a new one)...
...Fourth Division...
Second Division (another new one)...
....First Division....
...The Championship...

and finally

The Premiership

The Royals have been there, and done that!

In the non-League world (in the F.A.Cup)
they have experiences from Barking to Yeovil
and from Bridgwater to Blyth.

Now read on and enjoy over 130 of the stories

in

Reading versus The Rest

Aberdare Athletic

The

Biscuitmen

The 1923/24 season saw the club playing Aberdare Athletic, not only in the Third Division South, but also in the fifth qualifying round of the F.A.Cup, in December. Reading had already lost the two League games against the Welshmen back in October.

The Biscuitmen had at this time a miserable F.A.Cup record having already lost on their first attempt during each of the previous six seasons, therefore they must have gone into this game with great trepidation, and this attitude proved justified. Not only did they lose to their opponents (at the Ynys Stadium) by a single goal to nil, as had their two attempts earlier in the season, but their only recompense was a paltry sum of just under £30-00 as their share of the gate for their troubles. The official attendance was only 2,752 for a team that had been so optimistic - and well supported - when they first were elected to the Football League in 1921. In pouring rain, and with precious little cover for spectators it was little wonder that the locals didn't bother to turn out for the match.

The club's succession of Cup defeats came to an end the next year, and just three seasons later they reached the semi-final of the competition.

Accrington Stanley

The

Biscuitmen

Competition	Played (Total)	Home					Away					Total	
		W	D	L	F	A	W	D	L	F	A	F	A
League	4	2	0	0	7	0	0	1	1	3	4	10	4

~ *Playing Record* ~

Since the two clubs only met on four occasions (in League Division Three during the late 1950's) there is not much scope for finding anything particularly memorable within those few confrontations! Suffice it to say that the last game of the 1958/59 season saw The Biscuitmen thrash Stanley 5-0 at Elm Park, when Bobby Ayre scored a hat-trick, and long time favourite 'Jimmy' Wheeler netted a brace. The two also scored in the earlier match in Lancashire (as did Willie Gardiner - one of only two in total for the club), when Reading lost by the odd goal in seven. The end of season victory ensured the club a respectable final sixth place in the division. The next season Accrington were relegated, after their two seasons in the Third, and soon after resigned from the League.

Plymouth born William Smith, made only three appearances for Reading (in the 1947/48 season) before moving on to play for several other clubs, where his appearances were also infrequent. He ended his professional playing career at Peel Park, Accrington. At Stanley he had the dubious distinction of playing in their last ever Football League match. In 2006, a third club bearing the 'Accrington' name was promoted to the League.

Aldershot

The

Biscuitmen

~ Playing Record ~

Competition	Played	Home					Away					Total	
	(Total)	W	D	L	F	A	W	D	L	F	A	F	A
League	50	18	4	3	65	29	8	11	6	45	35	110	64
F.A.Cup	11	5	1	0	18	7	1	1	3	6	12	24	19

Aldershot didn't make their debut into the Football League until 1932, and that season was to be the first of many (around 50 League games) fought between the two local rivals. One of the most memorable of those many matches was in Aldershot's third season, the 1934/35, when The Biscuitmen were able to display their new goalscoring signing, Tommy Tait, who had just arrived from Bournemouth & Boscombe. The club were financially struggling at the time and would never have been able to pay the asked for transfer fee of £1,000 had it not been for the £200 contribution made by the supporters club.

But much of this was 'paid back' for the newcomer made a sensational debut for Reading scoring a hat-trick (and he also had two 'goals' disallowed) as the Shots were beaten 5-2 at the Recreation Ground. Tait went on to total 10 goals in his first seven games. He stayed for five years (during which time he was the first Reading player to be sent off at Elm Park), before leaving in 1939 on a free transfer to Torquay, but subsequently he returned for a spell as a Wartime guest player.

Aldershot, a generally struggling club throughout their career, finally folded in 1992 without completing their Division Four fixtures. But a later reincarnation - Aldershot Town - are on the sidelines to regain Football League membership for the Hampshire town.

Arsenal

~ Playing Record ~

Competition	Played (Total)	Home					Away					Total	
		W	D	L	F	A	W	D	L	F	A	F	A
League	2	0	0	1	0	4	0	0	1	1	2	1	6
F.A.Cup	3	0	0	3	2	6	0	0	0	0	0	2	6
League Cup	2	0	0	0	0	0	0	0	2	0	4	0	4

For a club never before met in the Football League prior to the 2006/07 season, over the years, the two teams were destined to play each other, almost, frequently in the two major cup competitions. Perhaps needless to say, the much higher rated Gunners always came out on top, with five victories, three in the F.A.Cup and two in the League Cup. But who would have dared hope that the pair, a few months later, would be meeting on League duty after the last occasion, in the Football League Cup, when Reading lost 3-0 at Highbury in November 2005.

The dream was soon realised when Arsenal were entertained at the Madejski Stadium, in front of the TV cameras on Sunday 22nd October 2006. But despite having made a respectable start to Premiership football (which very much improved as the season wore on), the newcomers to this level of football were no match for the rampaging Gunners. Henry gave them the lead after just one minute, and Hleb added a second just before the break. Another goal soon after half-time and the fourth before the end, ensured what was to become, by far, The Royals' worst defeat of the season.

A rare picture from the 1920's, of the Ynys Stadium ground of Aberdare Athletic, as it would have looked at the time of Reading's visit.

Jimmy Wheeler who netted a brace in the Accrington Stanley 5-0 victory.

The two captains, Ingimarsson and Henry, meet before the start of the first ever League match against Arsenal, in October 2006.

Sidwell's first of two goals versus Aston Villa.

Stuart Lovell who scored the match winner at Underhill, Barnet.

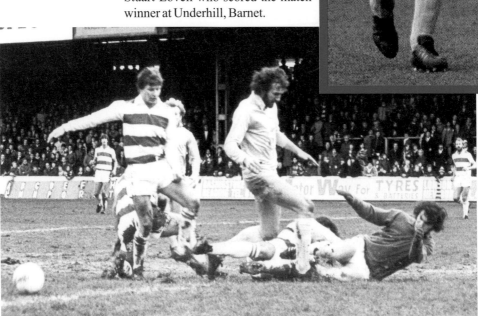

Goalkeeper Death is kept busy in the Barking F.A.Cup match.

Aston Villa

~ *Playing Record* ~

Competition	Played (Total)	Home					Away					Total	
		W	D	L	F	A	W	D	L	F	A	F	A
League	6	1	0	2	5	7	0	0	3	3	6	8	13
* F.A.Cup	2	0	0	1	1	3	0	0	1	1	5	2	8
League Cup	4	0	1	0	1	1	0	0	3	2	8	3	9

Until 2007, The Royals' record against Villa had made dismal reading with just one draw in 10 meetings in the League and cups. When the two teams met for the return Premiership match in February (Reading having lost their first ever away match in the Premiership at Villa Park in August 2006), things could surely only improve - and they did.

The attendance of 24,122 was a record at the Madejski Stadium, marginally the highest home gate of the season to that date, beating the numbers attracted to the Chelsea, Arsenal and Manchester United matches. Villa should have taken the lead early on, but it was Steve Sidwell who opened the account with a header after 16 minutes, in a period when the Royals were dominant. Villa came back strongly in the second half, with Ashley Young being the main culprit for missed chances, but as in the first half Reading dominated for half the second period. With referee, Mr. Clattenburg, looking at his watch to blow up for full time, Sidwell scored again following a brilliant interchange with Dave Kitson.

The 2-0 victory, and the team's consolidation in 6th place in the table, made up, in a large part, for the previous disappointing results over the Midlanders.

Barking

Competition	Played	Home					Away					Total	
	(Total)	W	D	L	F	A	W	D	L	F	A	F	A
F.A.Cup	1	1	0	0	3	1	0	0	0	0	0	3	1

~ Playing Record ~

The F.A.Cup provides the opportunity for Football League teams to meet clubs from the non-League world that otherwise would never be encountered. Barking on this occasion was the team, and Elm Park in the 1979/80 season was the time, at the second round stage.

Barking at this period were a leading non-League club, being members of the Isthmian League Premier Division, and that season was to prove to be quite successful for they finished seventh in their table of 22 clubs. They had already won a succession of four away games in the F.A.Cup, having started back at the first qualifying round stage, before meeting Oxford United at their own Mayesbrook Park ground. A surprising 1-0 victory over these other Third Division rivals meant that Reading could not take the opposition lightly.

But in the final event things went fairly smoothly, with single goals from Richie Bowman (penalty) and Lawrie Sanchez - surprisingly the only ones scored in the F.A.Cup by the pair in their Reading careers - and Gary Heale, sealed the victory, although the non-League team did notch up a consolation strike.

Reading had previously knocked out another non-League team, Kettering Town, in the first round, and they progressed through to the fourth round, where they lost at Swansea.

Barnet

Competition	Played (Total)	Home					Away					Total	
		W	D	L	F	A	W	D	L	F	A	F	A
League	2	1	0	0	4	1	1	0	0	1	0	5	1

~ Playing Record ~

Reading and Barnet have only met on two competitive occasions over a period of 87 years, but the results of both these matches were to be a significant factor in the fortunes of Reading that season.

The first of the two meetings was on the 1st of September 1993, Barnet having just been promoted to Division Two. Reading had made a reasonable start to the season, having won two of their three opening League matches, and had a fairly easy time of this match, comfortably beating their visitors by 4-1 at Elm Park. The attendance of 4,971 was the lowest of the season, but subsequent results soon led to an improvement in home crowds.

By the return match, in April, the two clubs destinies were fairly defined. Although Reading's fine form had slipped over the previous weeks with them having lost three of their six League fixtures in March. But they came back at Underhill, albeit by the margin of only one goal, scored by Stuart Lovell, one of the two prolific goalscorers that season (the other being Jimmy Quinn). The double over Barnet produced six points, and a few weeks later Reading were hailed as Champions, by just one point ahead of Port Vale. At the other end of the table, Barnet finished bottom by eight clear points and were relegated.

Barnsley

The **Biscuitmen**

Even with over 50 League games to choose from, there are three - over a wide time span - that come to obvious prominence.

The first was in the 1930/31 season when Reading met fellow relegation strugglers Barnsley at Elm Park in late March. Heads must have dropped when the visitors took the lead, but they were soon lifted when Reading stormed away to win by 6-1; but it was all to no avail as they were eventually relegated whilst the Yorkshiremen survived.

Thirty-one years later it was a similar scenario, and another home game played in March. For Reading the future looked bleak as they had been languishing in the lower reaches of the table for three months. But a very welcome victory - comprehensively again - this time by 4-1, lifted the team. At the end of the season both teams escaped relegation.

In the 1979/80 season the circumstances were more relaxed, both teams experiencing mediocre seasons. In late December, Barnsley were the visitors, and they met Reading on the back of a dreadful run for The Royals of five games without a win, including a 7-1 thrashing at Chesterfield. But the homesters answered in the best way with a spectacular seven goal victory without reply. A newspaper headline read: "7 Up and Barnsley Bitter."

Barrow

~ Playing Record ~

Competition	Played	Home					Away					Total	
	(Total)	W	D	L	F	A	W	D	L	F	A	F	A
League	8	3	0	1	10	4	0	3	1	2	3	12	7

22nd January 1972, Reading versus Barrow. It was the middle of an indifferent season in the lowly Fourth Division for The Biscuitmen, whilst their opponents were having another miserable season which was ultimately to lead to them being voted out of the League at the next re-election meeting. Hardly the recipe for a bumper gate, but with the attendance numbering 11,689 it was by far the biggest League gate of the season which only averaged a lowly 5,531 that campaign. There was of course a reason for this anomaly.

Reading had reached the fourth round of the F.A.Cup after a fairly easy route in the previous three, having beaten fellow lowly neighbours Aldershot and two non-League teams. But what a draw in the next tie! Nothing less than the mighty Arsenal at home. Naturally the match was made an all-ticket affair, and these were made available prior to the Barrow match.

The roads around Elm Park were packed that afternoon, with queues forming all round, and 27,000 'fans' were rewarded with a ticket at twice the normal price. As for the Barrow match nearly 12,000 decided to stay on and pay to see this game, when a 1-0 home win (a goal from Les Chappell), put another nail in Barrow's coffin.

Barry Town

Competition	Played (Total)	Home					Away					Total	
		W	D	L	F	A	W	D	L	F	A	F	A
F.A.Cup	1	0	0	0	0	0	1	0	0	2	1	2	1

~ Playing Record ~

In 1984, Reading made a rare trip into Wales for an F.A.Cup tie. Whilst supporters were used to seeing the likes of Newport County and Swansea, this was a one-off versus another club from the south of the principality, Barry Town.

The Welshman previously had ambitions of joining the Football League, applying for the first time way back in 1921 and again in 1947. By the mid 1980's they had dropped down from the Southern to the Welsh League. But this was a cup match that could produce the potential 'banana skin' tie, for the non-Leaguers had already played six games in the competition - starting in the 1st qualifying round - and were riding high on their way to their League Championship.

A crowd of 4,000 packed into the somewhat dilapidated Jenner Park ground on the 17th of November, but true to form the favourites won 2-1, but only thanks to a last minute winner from Trevor Senior, the first goal coming from another Elm Park favourite Stuart Beavon. Twelve years later, Barry Town made headlines when they reached further than any other Welsh club in the UEFA Cup, negotiating two preliminary rounds before losing to Aberdeen.

(Top) Heale scores one of the seven goals versus Barnsley.

(Left) Les Chappell, who scored the only goal against Barrow.

(Below) A header from Love, of Barry Town, levels the score at 1-1 in the 1984 F.A.Cup match.

A cartoon captures the incidents from the Cup match against Bedford Town.

Steve Wood was one of the goalscorers in the 4-0 victory over Blackburn.

Wagstaff scores one of the goals at Blyth Spartans.

Bedford Town

The

Biscuitmen

Competition	Played	Home					Away					Total	
	(Total)	W	D	L	F	A	W	D	L	F	A	F	A
F.A.Cup	1	1	0	0	1	0	0	0	0	0	0	1	0

~ Playing Record ~

Viewed again over fifty years later, an F.A. Cup-tie, at home to a Southern League team in 1956 may not seem too difficult. But in Bedford Town, Reading were competing against one of the all-time famous giant-killers. Just a year earlier they had fought their way through from the first qualifying round - playing five games and scoring 21 goals with only one conceded. In the second round they beat Watford at home, and then sensationally held Arsenal to a 2-2 draw at Highbury (having fought back from 2-0 down and nearly scoring the winners in the last minute). In the replay they lost 2-1 but only after extra time.

The players and supporters could hardly have relished the visit of such a team to Elm Park one year later, and in the second round an enormous crowd of 22,895 (over three times the previous home League match attendance) tentatively greeted the team when they ran out on to the pitch. Fortunately for Reading there was to be no giant-killing this year, although it could have happened for the visiting 'Eagles' team did have a goal disallowed. But Reading proceeded courtesy of a single strike from ex-Scottish International Bobby Campbell, his only goal in fifteen matches in the competition for the club.

Birmingham City

~ Playing Record ~

Competition	Played (Total)	Home					Away					Total	
		W	D	L	F	A	W	D	L	F	A	F	A
League	16	1	5	2	8	9	2	3	3	8	14	16	23
F.A.Cup	4	1	1	0	2	1	1	0	1	4	4	6	5

There have been a number of battles with the Midlands team over the years, particularly in the F.A.Cup, and their encounter in the 1992/93 season was memorable for several completely different reasons.

Birmingham City were members of the, then, First Division (second tier), therefore why were they playing in the first round? For this single season, it was only the promoted Champions from the previous season (Brentford) that were given the traditional bye through to the third round. Also memorable was the fact that Reading managed to overcome their higher rated opponents, winning 1-0 in front of the Sky cameras (they went on to the third round where they lost in a replay to Manchester City). But probably that most likely to stir the memory was the starting line-up debut of 17 year-old James Lambert. The display of the youngster stunned the television audience, including Arsene Wenger who immediately invited him to train with his AC Monaco team for several days. And this exercise was soon repeated at Blackburn Rovers under the watchful eye of Kenny Dalgish. Yet, undoubtably brilliant on his day, he never completely fulfilled the promise shown, with a single appearance for the Football League against their Italian counterparts in 1995 being his only 'cap'.

Bishop Stortford

The

Biscuitmen

Competition	Played	Home					Away					Total	
	(Total)	W	D	L	F	A	W	D	L	F	A	F	A
F.A.Cup	2	1	0	1	7	3	0	0	0	0	0	7	3

~ *Playing Record* ~

The F.A.Cup provides the occasional opportunity for a League team to meet a non-League one in the same competition, but this club have been encountered twice, and on both occasions at Elm Park; but what a contrast the two results produced.

In the 1970/71 season, The Biscuitmen were having a fairly uncomfortable time of it in the Third Division, apart from their two consecutive victories immediately prior to the first round of the Cup. The adverse results had included three games when four goals were conceded and one of five. But in the F.A.Cup, things went pretty much to plan, and it was the League team that were rampant, for Bishop Stortford were comfortably dispatched 6-1, with Les Chappell netting a hat-trick. Reading later left the competition after losing 5-0 at Watford, and at the end of the season they were relegated to the Fourth Division.

Eleven years later, and now back in the Third Division, the Reading cup -tie against the same opposition, saw the non-Leaguers enjoy a totally different match, for they produced the shock result of the first round when they won 2-1 at Elm Park (to date, Reading's only home game reverse in the Cup to a non-League team) This club could be considered an unlucky omen, for come the season's end, once again Reading were relegated!

Blackburn Rovers

~ Playing Record ~

Competition	Played	Home					Away					Total	
	(Total)	W	D	L	F	A	W	D	L	F	A	F	A
League	8	1	2	1	6	3	0	3	1	6	8	12	11
* F.A.Cup													

In all honesty, it is difficult to find a really 'memorable' occasion involving Reading and the Lancashire side, for the encounters between the two are fairly rare. There was a pre-First World War F.A.Cup clash with these illustrious opponents (outside the timescale of this book), but until 2006, only six Football League encounters, four of which ended in draws. Apart from their two meetings in the 1979/80 season (when Blackburn were at a low ebb in the Third Division), the other matches were in the (old) Second Division days in the mid-1980's.

Promoted as Third Divisions champions in 1986, Reading entertained the Rovers early in the 1986/87 season, whilst a few months earlier the visitors had only narrowly avoided relegation to that same tier. The Royals had made only a modest start to the campaign, but the result against Blackburn promised (albeit unfulfilled) good times ahead. Single goals by Paul Canoville, Trevor Senior, Steve Wood and Kevin Bremner ensured a comprehensive 4-0 victory, in what transpired to be the best result of the season. Yet, ironically, the attendance of 6,001, was one of the lowest. The return game at Ewood Park in April, true to form, produced a goalless draw!

Blackpool

The
Biscuitmen

Competition	Played	Home					Away					Total	
	(Total)	W	D	L	F	A	W	D	L	F	A	F	A
League	30	7	6	2	21	9	5	3	7	19	27	40	36

~ Playing Record ~

Whilst there are many matches to choose from (30), personnel between the clubs perhaps are more significant. The most prominent was Joe Smith.

Relegation at the end of the 1930/31 season led to the resignation of manager Angus Wylie, and the subsequent appointment of the untried, but well respected former Bolton Wanderers and England International Joe Smith; his initial salary was £8 per week. Smith's four seasons in charge were hardly poor ones, for on each occasion the club came close to promotion, but this was not enough to satisfy one element at the club, and eventually they reluctantly accepted his resignation in the Summer of 1935.

Smith took over at Blackpool, where he became one of the most successful managers of all time. He took the club back into the First Division, and was in charge of the team at the famous 'Matthews Final' of 1953. He also guided the club to the First Division runners-up spot in 1956.

In the other direction, former Blackpool player, and wartime guest at Elm Park, Harry Johnston, joined Reading as manager in 1955. Popular with fans and players alike, at seven years he became the longest serving manager at Reading to date, especially significant since these were years of financial problems at Elm Park.

Blyth Spartans

~ Playing Record ~

Competition	Played (Total)	Home					Away					Total	
		W	D	L	F	A	W	D	L	F	A	F	A
F.A.Cup	2	1	0	0	6	1	0	1	0	2	2	8	3

For several reasons this F.A.Cup-tie in 1971 had its highs and lows. The north-easterners had already disposed of Crewe Alexandra (away) and Stockport County at home to reach the third round stage. Having to make the long journey, and under the charge of a new manager, Reading must have been looking to the game with some trepidation.

This caution was well founded for the Amateurs who were a powerful force in the Northern League, fought back to hold the League team to a 2-2 draw, before a capacity crowd of 6,800. Blyth's Croft Park ground had seen better days, and this opinion had already been voiced by The Biscuitmen. As if in retaliation, Blyth refused to play under Reading's (perfectly satisfactory for Football League matches) floodlights. The game therefore kicked-off at 2.15 p.m. and in the circumstances this would have produced a poor gate, but as the fourth round offered a home match versus Arsenal for the victors the attendance of 10,550 was very good - around double the normal League crowd.

Reading were easy winners in the replay, crushing the opposition 6-1, which included a Peter Harman hat-trick, who in the previous round had first opened his account for Reading, scoring the winner against Aldershot.

Bognor Regis Town

The Royals

Competition	Played	Home					Away					Total	
	(Total)	W	D	L	F	A	W	D	L	F	A	F	A
F.A.Cup	1	1	0	0	6	2	0	0	0	0	0	6	2

~ Playing Record ~

The fates would seem to throw Reading up against non-League Clubs with the initial letter 'B' in the F.A. Cup, this Sussex side being one of eight in the 'set'. Another 'B' had already been played, against Barry Town in the first round that season, 1984/85

The second round game was played at Elm Park, where The Royals totally dominated their Isthmian League opponents with a 6-2 scoreline, despite the non-Leaguers highly merited replay victory over Swansea City in the first round. The Reading goalscorers were, the almost inevitable Trevor Senior (with two), a pair from Ian Juryeff (his only goals for the club in a short loan period), Mark White (also his only Reading F.A.Cup goal) and Stuart Beavon. That same day Stirling Albion beat Selkirk 20-0 in a Scottish Cup-tie.

Just a month earlier an overall disappointing season had seen fewer than 2,800 turn out for the home League match versus Leyton Orient, therefore the crowd of 6,606 against relatively unattractive opposition was seen as good (the average crowd in League matches that season was one of the worst ever, a paltry 3,689, the sixth lowest in the Third Division).

Reading were knocked out of the next round by Barnsley, the third 'B' that season!

Bolton Wanderers

Despite the final heart-break, the 1995 play-off Final must surely be the most memorable match

~ Playing Record ~

Competition	Played	Home					Away					Total	
	(Total)	W	D	L	F	A	W	D	L	F	A	F	A
# League	20	6	1	2	15	8	2	2	6	10	17	25	25
* F.A.Cup	1	0	0	0	0	0	0	0	1	0	2	0	2

Finishing second in the First Division, only Bolton stood in the way of the club's greatest achievement - promotion to the Premiership. At Wembley in front of 64,107 (over half from Reading) the team made a dream start to the play-off final taking a two goal lead after only 12 minutes through Lee Nogan and Adrian Williams. The over physical Bolton side were justly punished when a penalty was awarded for a foul on Michael Gilkes. The chance of taking a three goal lead after only 27 minutes, led the fans into dreaming of Old Trafford and Highbury. But Stuart Lovell's spot kick was well saved, before he then blasted the rebound over the bar.

The second half took its toll on the not fully fit Reading team, and their opponents hit back with fifteen minutes on the clock, and then a devastating equaliser after 86. From a comfortable lead the exhausted team now had to try and take the advantage again, but it wasn't to be, for two more Bolton goals sealed their fate, despite a late consolation from Jimmy Quinn.

A crushing end to the season, and the club had to wait 11 years for that ultimate promotion.

Boston United

Competition	Played (Total)	Home					Away					Total	
		W	D	L	F	A	W	D	L	F	A	F	A
League Cup	1	0	0	0	0	0	1	0	0	3	1	3	1

Reading have never met The Pilgrims on Football League duty, the Lincolnshire club having only been promoted to this level in 2002, by which time The Royals were already in the Championship. Without any clashes in the F.A.Cup, it was only a single game in the League Cup when the two met.

Boston United rose to Football League status relatively rapidly, and in fact the only real success they had in cup competitions was their reaching the F.A.Trophy Final (the non-League cup for more Senior clubs) in 1985. Their first attempt at the Football League Cup coincided with their first season in the Football League, of course, and after a 2-0 debut victory over Bristol Rovers, they lost 5-1 at home to Cardiff City.

The match against Reading came the following season, 2003/04, the first competitive game of the campaign, and despite the chance of seeing a newly promoted team, two levels above their own, only 2,055 spectators were enticed to the compact York Street Ground. Nicky Forster gave The Royals a half-time lead, but this was cancelled out when they conceded a penalty in the second period. It was only two late goals, by Steve Sidwell and another from Forster, that allowed the team to progress on to the second round.

Bournemouth (AFC)

The

Biscuitmen

~ Playing Record ~

Competition	Played (Total)	Home					Away					Total	
		W	D	L	F	A	W	D	L	F	A	F	A
League	100	30	9	11	93	54	11	15	24	48	70	141	124
F.A.Cup	3	1	0	0	1	0	0	0	2	0	3	1	3
League Cup	2	0	0	1	1	3	0	0	1	0	2	1	5

Bournemouth hold the record for the team most often met in competitive matches with a round 100 in the Football League, yet on only four occasions have the two met in the major cups to date.

Two matches, not within these numbers, were reserve team fixtures. Near the end of the 1947/48 season, crowds were at all time highs, and fans also flocked to see the reserves with a record attendance of 8,241 set for the visit of the 'Spurs second team. Yet just a few weeks later this was eclipsed with 10,815 present when visitors Bournemouth visited Elm Park in the Combination Cup semi-final.

In later years there has occasionally been keen interest taken in the reserves, particularly so at the end of the 1965/66 season. Challenging for promotion from the Combination Second Division, the team went on to finish with an unbeaten 17 game run. Support was such that the match at Oxford United saw the Supporters Club run coaches to the game, and over 300 made the short journey to support the reserves at Aldershot. A point was needed to clinch the Championship, and at home to Bournemouth this was duly achieved, before a 5,142 crowd (which didn't include season ticket holders that were present), Denis Allen scoring a late equaliser in the 1-1 draw.

Goalkeeper Shaka Hislop was one of the heroes in the most memorable and heart-breaking of matches - versus Bolton at Wembley.

Just one competitive game has been played versus shortlived Football League club Boston United.

Jimmy Wheeler with the Championship Shield won by the reserves after their victory over Bournemouth.

(left) Reading favourite Johnny Walker who scored his only goal of the season versus Bradford (Park Avenue).

(below) Chappell comes close at the Brentwood Town Cup game.

Five notable personalities from the first premiership season, (top) Hunt, Ingimarsson (bottom) Sonko, Coppell and Sodje - all ex-Brentford!

Bradford City

~ Playing Record ~

Competition	Played	Home					Away					Total	
	(Total)	W	D	L	F	A	W	D	L	F	A	F	A
League	50	9	10	6	30	27	8	4	13	34	49	64	76
* F.A.Cup													
League Cup	6	0	3	0	3	3	0	1	2	2	4	5	7

The 1984/85 season was one of those strange ones that probably come to every club at some time - a better 'away' record than that at 'home'. Thirty-eight points on their travels and only thirty-one at home was one such season for Reading. Amongst the eleven victories won away from Elm Park, the most satisfying was at Bradford City.

On the 4th of May, and with four games to play, the Yorkshire team was strolling away with the Third Division Championship, whereas Reading had to be content with a just above mid-table final finish. For the Valley Parade team a few more points were needed to guarantee promotion whilst their opponents had nothing to lose. Perhaps it was this scenario that led to the shock result of the season for both clubs, when Reading thrashed their opponents 5-2, with goals from David Crown, Martin Hicks (2), Dean Horrix, and Mark White. It was in fact the third time in which the team had been involved in the scoring of five goals in one League match that season, with a 5-1 home thrashing of Burnley and the same score defeat at Lincoln.

A far greater tragedy for the Bradford public came at that club's next home game, when 53 fans lost their life in the infamous fire at Valley Parade.

Bradford (Park Avenue)

The

Biscuitmen

There were just ten competitive matches played against the Yorkshire club (who were voted out of the League in 1970). One notable meeting was in fact the first (prior to the period covered in this book), when the newly formed team from Yorkshire played their first ever first team match, against Reading, in the Southern League in 1907/08. The ambitious Park Avenue opted for the geographically strange Southern League since they felt this was the strongest competition outside the League itself, yet their reserves played at the opposite end of the country, in the North-Eastern League!

In the disastrous 1930/31 season, one very minor bright spot was The Biscuitmen's only away victory of the season, at Park Avenue, where the Bradford team only lost two League games that season. The home match was also won, therefore this represented the only 'double' of the season. Reading were relegated at the end of the season.

The two clubs didn't meet again until the 1961/62 season, in the Third Division, when once again the 'double' (both 3-1 scores) was achieved. One of the goals, a penalty, was scored by one of Reading's 'Greats', popular captain and full-back Johnny Walker, his only one of the season.

Brentford

~ Playing Record ~

Competition	Played (Total)	Home					Away					Total	
		W	D	L	F	A	W	D	L	F	A	F	A
# League	76	22	10	6	72	36	9	12	17	45	63	117	99
* F.A.Cup	3	3	0	0	9	2	0	0	0	0	0	9	2
League Cup	2	0	1	0	1	1	0	0	1	0	2	1	3

Having played against Brentford in no fewer than 76 League matches plus games in other major competitions, there are many recollections that could be considered, but perhaps the most striking are the personnel themselves that have moved from one club to the other, and those that contributed towards the club's elevation and holding of Premiership status.

Starting at the top was manager Steve Coppell, who enjoyed a fairly short but successful period at the Brentford helm and coach Wally Downes who had a not so successful period in the hot seat that followed. Five former Bees moved on to become Reading players in a fairly short space of time, and eventually rose to Premiership status, namely: Steven Hunt (a Coppell free signing from Crystal Palace), Ivar Ingirmarsson (a £150,000 signing in 1999 from Iceland) Steve Sidwell (a one season 18 year-old loanee from Arsenal), Sam Sodje (a flamboyant signing from non-League Margate) and Ibrahima Sonko (another favourite during his time at Griffin Park).

With those players and staff still at the club, the Griffin Park supporters must consider that it could have been them, rather than their neighbours up the M4 that could have become one of the leading clubs in the early 21st century.

Brentwood Town

The

Biscuitmen

It was a somewhat troubled and apprehensive team that travelled to Essex in November 1969, to The Hive and the home of Southern League club Brentwood Town. Reading were finding goals hard to come by and their mediocre performances were not appreciated by the fans. The F.A.Cup result that followed did nothing to allay these fears. Their opponents had only entered the competition at the fourth qualifying round stage, based on their performances a year earlier when they reached the second round (only to lose 10-1 at Southend).

3,047 spectators packed into the little ground, and most of them erupted when Halliday for the home team scored. This goal was the only one of the game, and Reading had failed, following a well below par performance, at the hands of a non-League team.

This was destined to be Brentwood's penultimate F.A.Cup match (they lost in the second round to Northampton before a record gate), for at the end of the season they vacated The Hive and technically merged with Chelmsford City.

Meanwhile things got worse before they got better at Reading, as they lost their next match 6-2 at Southport but recovered sufficiently to finish 8th in the Third Division that season.

Bridgwater Town

Competition	Played	Home					Away					Total	
	(Total)	W	D	L	F	A	W	D	L	F	A	F	A
F.A.Cup	1	0	0	0	0	0	1	0	0	3	0	3	0

~ Playing Record ~

The main headline preceding this F.A.Cup match against non-League opposition in the 1971/72 season was the debut of Andy Proudlove, at just 16 years 309 days, the youngest ever to represent Reading in a competitive first team game (three weeks later Steve Hetzke took over this record, but Proudlove remains to date the youngest Reading player in the F.A.Cup). This was Andy's only claim to fame, for he appeared in only five League matches for the club (one as sub.) before moving on to several other Football League sides, but never becoming a regular at any.

Conversely, Hetzke eventually became a long term favourite at Elm Park, initially as a central defender, then as a striker. Latterly, back in his defending role he achieved the final accolade by being made club captain in the 1981/82 season. With over 300 first team appearances to his credit, he moved on to other clubs, and in total increased this number by nearly 50%.

At Bridgwater the team was under the charge of caretaker manager, Jimmy Wallbanks, a former player and trainer. Predictably the team won (3-0) before progressing on to the 4th round, and an Elm Park date with Arsenal.

Brighton and Hove Albion

The

Biscuitmen

Having played the Sussex team so many times - despite the two never having met in the F.A.Cup - there are many game options to choose from. In a few of these, high scoring matches were a feature, except in the four League Cup fixtures, when just five goals in total have been netted.

During the 1940/41 season (although not statistically included above), in the opening home (Wartime) London League match Reading won 5-4 (with the visitors using six guest players from Liverpool), after having lost their first match at Clapton Orient by 8-3. Three years later (in the Football League South) they crushed Albion 9-3 on their own Goldstone Road ground.

The boot was on the other foot in the last 'away' match of the 1956/57 season, when the team was at the end of an 8-3 drubbing. In the 1962/63 season a rare mid-Winter match was played at Elm Park (horrendous weather that season saw the team play no matches in January and only two in February). The enforced lay-off obviously didn't suit the home team for they lost by the odd goal in nine (earlier in the season they had come away from Brighton with a 4-2 victory).

Bristol City

The

Biscuitmen

~ Playing Record ~

Competition	Played (Total)	Home					Away					Total	
		W	D	L	F	A	W	D	L	F	A	F	A
League	76	18	10	10	64	58	10	6	22	46	82	110	140
* F.A.Cup													
League Cup	2	0	1	0	2	2	1	0	0	3	2	5	4

Over the years, a number of players have played for both clubs, amongst them are:

Dean Horrix, who came to Reading from Millwall, and later moved on to Bristol City. But tragically just ten days after signing for The Robins he was killed in a car crash. Wally Hinshelwood after 143 games for Reading moved to Bristol City in 1956 for £5,500, and was a first team regular at Ashton Gate for four years. George Marks guested for Reading, from Arsenal, during the second World War, but when he was formally transferred to Elm Park (in a player exchange with Vic Barney), in October 1948, he was a Bristol City player. A wartime England International, he was Reading's first choice goalkeeper until December 1950.

Vic Barney signed for The Biscuitmen, and was drafted into the team for the club's record 10-2 victory over Crystal Palace in August 1946, before moving to Ashton Gate two years later. Bobby Williams started his League career at Bristol City and ended it at Reading in 1969. After a spell in non-League football he was appointed the reserve team manager in 1976, then in the same role with the Youth team, before moving back to Bristol City as a Youth Scout. Finally, he returned to Reading as a Scout!

Bristol Rovers

The Biscuitmen

~ Playing Record ~

Competition	Played (Total)	Home					Away					Total	
		W	D	L	F	A	W	D	L	F	A	F	A
League	80	25	5	10	74	46	8	12	20	45	70	119	116
* F.A.Cup	5	1	1	1	4	4	1	1	0	2	1	6	5
League Cup	4	2	0	1	10	5	1	0	0	2	1	12	6

When Rovers entertained Reading in the opening match of the 1939/40 season, little was it realised that this would be the club's last 'away' match in the Football League for six years, due to the normal football programme closing down during the War. In the 1946/47 season the first fixture from 1939 was repeated, the score was the same at 2-2, and MacPhee netted one for Reading in both matches.

In the first of these two games, there had been five players making their debuts: Wilf Chitty (who scored the other goal) and also appeared in the 1946 game. Joe Wilson, who made his only three appearances for the club that season plus Alf Fenwick and Ernie Whittam for whom this was their only games.

Finally, Maurice Edelston, who hardly needs any introduction was the fifth new member in 1939. One of Reading's all time great players, he signed for the club in 1939 as an Amateur, combined his playing role with that of club secretary for a short period after the war, but finally left the club for Northampton in 1952. There is no doubt he would have added to his 355 appearances (including those in Wartime) had it not been for the intervention of the hostilities.

Bromley

The

Biscuitmen

~ Playing Record ~

Competition	Played	Home				Away				Total	
	(Total)	W	D	L	F	A	W	D	L	F	A	F	A
F.A.Cup	2	1	0	0	3	0	0	1	0	3	3	6	3

Reading's one competitive match (two games) against Bromley was in the F.A.Cup, of course. The 1947/48 season was only the second post-War normal season, and football was enjoying a boom in peacetime Britain. The Hayes Lane ground, which the Amateurs had only occupied since 1938, was packed with an 8,700 crowd, and the locals were looking for a shock result, which very nearly came to pass. An exciting match saw the Athenian League side hanging on to a single goal lead until a late equaliser from winger Chris Bertschin, his debut goal for the club with whom he had only recently turned professional.

This season extra time was played in first meetings, and during this period, Reading twice took the lead, but the tenacious Amateurs fought back each time to force a 3-3 draw. The replay at Elm Park took place on the following Saturday, and watched by 15,257 spectators the game went as expected. Bromley were no match for their Football League counterparts, who strolled away with a 3-0 victory. Those on target were Ronnie Dix (who in 1928 and aged 15 years and 180 days became the Football League's youngest ever goalscorer), winger Freddy Fisher and the club's all-time record goalscorer Tony MacPhee.

Burnley

The

Biscuitmen

~ Playing Record ~

Competition	Played	Home				Away					Total	
	(Total)	W	D	L	F	A	W	D	L	F	A	F	A
League	26	6	6	1	21	11	6	3	4	18	23	39	34
* F.A.Cup	3	1	1	0	4	3	0	0	1	0	1	4	4
League Cup	1	0	0	1	1	2	0	0	0	0	0	1	2

It's more palatable to read about the Reading F.C. positives, but equally one has to be objective, and that is the case with this chosen Burnley match.

The 1930/31 (relegation) season in the Second Division had started disastrously with an awful (near record) 7-1 defeat at Tottenham, and by the time the team travelled to Turf Moor on September the 13th, they had lost their opening five League matches, with an awful goal difference of three for and eighteen against. Record signing Frank Eaton was at least earning his fee having scored all three (he went on to record the first five, and with 15 was the second top goalscorer that season). But could it get worse. Yes!

The match at Burnley was a humiliating defeat of 8-1, the club's all time record adverse score in the Football League. However, there was some excuse, for surprisingly the visitors were on top for the first 20 minutes and it looked as if something could be gained from the game. But when ex-Manchester United goalkeeper Lance Richardson was injured, things took a turn for the worst. Later, Richardson (there were three players with this surname at the club at the time) had to go off injured, and the goals just kept raining in.

Flanagan scores at Bridgwater Town.

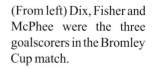

An all-time great, Maurice Edelston, who was in the team versus Bristol Rovers in 1939.

(From left) Dix, Fisher and McPhee were the three goalscorers in the Bromley Cup match.

(Cardiff City) Reading 'keeper, Duckworth, is unable to stop The Bluebirds scoring the second goal.

Carnaby scored his only goal of the season at Cambridge United.

(Charlton Athletic) Adie Williams (partly hidden) scores the winner - whilst Lee Nogan looks on.

Bury

~ Playing Record ~

Competition	Played	Home					Away					Total	
	(Total)	W	D	L	F	A	W	D	L	F	A	F	A
League	46	9	6	8	35	35	4	5	14	22	43	57	78
F.A.Cup	2	0	1	0	1	1	0	0	1	0	3	1	4
League Cup	1	1	0	0	2	1	0	0	0	0	0	2	1

Older fans will say that in 'the old days', matches were finished even on waterlogged pitches with water over the ankles, an exaggeration perhaps, but the abandonment of the Coca Cola (League) Cup match at home to Bury on the 24th of October 1995 was certainly controversial.

The struggling visitors from the Third Division, had shocked First Division Reading after taking an early two goal lead. Then, after 28 minutes, referee John Kirkby brought proceedings to an end by abandoning the game (hence the shortest 'match' in Reading's history). The Bury contingent were incensed, claiming that the home officials had done nothing or little to prevent puddles forming on the waterlogged pitch. The game was replayed two weeks later, and Bury players Kelly and Stant made their point by running onto the pitch clutching pitchforks!

The replayed game ran to form, but only just. An own goal and one from Jimmy Quinn eased The Royals through to the fourth round. Reading went on to beat Southampton, before losing to Leeds United, and despite this good run in the Cup, they struggled in the League, coming close to relegation. Meanwhile, Bury recovered from their Cup disappointment and later were promoted to the Second Division.

Cambridge United

~ Playing Record ~

Competition	Played (Total)	Home W	D	L	F	A	Away W	D	L	F	A	Total F	A
League	20	8	2	0	17	4	2	3	5	10	17	27	21
F.A.Cup	2	0	0	1	1	2	0	1	0	0	0	1	2
League Cup	3	0	0	1	0	3	0	0	2	1	4	1	7

The most dramatic match of the League games with Cambridge was that, late in the 1975/76 season. This was The Royals fifth season in the basement division, too long in the fans' eyes. After drawing with already promoted Lincoln City at Elm Park before their biggest Fourth Division attendance, and another at home to Brentford, just one point was needed at the Abbey Stadium, Cambridge, to clinch promotion.

Meanwhile mid-table United had nothing to play for and therefore there was no pressure on their young players. But it was the visitors who took the lead after only two minutes from the mercurial Robin Friday. However, the celebrations at the away end were shortlived, for Cambridge drew level just three minutes later. Friday was involved again on 13 minutes when his play left Bryan Carnaby free to slot in the winner, ironically his only goal of the season. The play continued at a frantic pace, before Reading's chances were boosted with the sending off of Cambridge's Batson. Yet it was the home side that fought back and scored an equaliser.

But it was all celebrations in the Reading camp, for with one match still to play (Crewe were beaten at Elm Park) promotion had been realised, the first for 50 years!

Cardiff City

The
Biscuitmen

~ Playing Record ~

Competition	Played (Total)	Home					Away					Total	
		W	D	L	F	A	W	D	L	F	A	F	A
League	42	11	6	4	41	18	7	4	10	27	42	68	60
F.A.Cup	4	0	>1	0	1	1	1	1	$1	3	5	4	6
League Cup	2	0	0	0	0	0	0	0	2	2	10	2	10

The 1927 F.A.Cup Final is especially remembered in that the only club outside England - Cardiff City - were the winners, when they beat Arsenal. Not so well publicised, is the fact that Reading appeared opposite the Welsh team in the semi-final.

It took Reading nine matches to reach this stage, including two replays against Manchester United, the record attendance at Elm Park when Brentford were beaten, and a 3-1 win at Swansea. Despite Cardiff's pedigree as a First Division club, the second Division Berkshire team felt they were in with a good chance, but they never really got started and a 25th minute strike by Ferguson, followed with a headed goal eight minutes later, all but dashed their hopes. With eight internationals in their line-up the Welsh Bluebirds were unshakeable despite the enthusiasm and effort put in by Reading, but the match was all but over when Ferguson added another goal in the second half.

The match had produced terrific support from the town, including 7,000 who travelled on special trains to Molineux, Wolverhampton, while far greater numbers listened to the radio commentary - the first semi-final to be broadcast - at home. They may have lost the match, but this long F.A.Cup run would forever remain in the memory of supporters as one of the club's greatest achievements.

Carlisle United

Competition	Played	Home					Away					Total	
	(Total)	W	D	L	F	A	W	D	L	F	A	F	A
League	10	3	1	1	10	5	1	3	1	7	7	17	12

~ *Playing Record* ~

The Royals have only met Carlisle, from this far North-west football outpost, on a few occasions in the League and never in the cups, and none of these games were significantly memorable.

Carlisle were first encountered in the 1962/63 season, when, by October, Reading were looking possible relegation candidates, despite a 5-0 opening of the season victory over Shrewsbury. By the end of September just three more victories and eight defeats had been experienced.

Two wins followed in October, before Harry Johnston was allowed to spend large sums of money on two new players - a record £11,000 to West Ham for Ron Tindall, and another £6,000 when Arsenal parted with Johnny Petts. It looked as if this was to be the key to turning around the club's fortunes, for they both made their debut at home to Carlisle on the 12th of October and a morale boosting 2-0 victory was the result. But far from it, for the club were soon hovering around the relegation zone again, finally escaping the 'drop' by just two places and four points. Carlisle, meanwhile, were not so lucky, for they finished second from bottom of the Third Division. The two clubs soon met again, two seasons later, following Carlisle's promotion from the Fourth.

Charlton Athletic

The

Biscuitmen

~ *Playing Record* ~

Competition	Played (Total)	Home					Away					Total	
		W	D	L	F	A	W	D	L	F	A	F	A
League	30	8	5	2	24	14	4	4	7	12	19	36	33
League Cup	2	0	1	0	2	2	0	0	1	1	3	3	5

There have been several instances involving this south-east London club that have influenced the fortunes of Reading.

The first involved a player, in 1931. Sam Bartram was a half-back who never made it into the Reading first team and was allowed to move on to Charlton. He was converted into a goalkeeper, and then enjoyed a long and famous career lasting over twenty years at The Valley. Still in the pre-war days (1934/35), the two clubs met at the top of Division Three South just before Christmas. Despite arriving late at The Valley, Reading took the lead, before a succession of injuries, a disputed equaliser and two late efforts sealed a 3-1 defeat. Charlton were promoted, and The Biscuitmen finished second (only one promotion place at that time).

Sixty years later the two clubs met in the last game of the season, when a 2-1 home victory decided Reading's runners-up final placing (a re-arrangement of the divisions dictated that only one team - again - were promoted that season!). Finally, in the 2001/02 season, it was a player who was a significant factor. Loan signing John Salako, from Charlton, had a major influence on The Royals' run of 11 unbeaten games from late December, during which time the former England player scored in the first three games.

Chelsea

Competition	Played (Total)	Home W	D	L	F	A	Away W	D	L	F	A	Total F	A
		~ Playing Record ~											
League	10	2	1	2	9	8	0	3	2	3	5	12	13
F.A.Cup	3	0	1	0	0	0	0	0	1	1	3	3	5
League Cup	3	1	0	1	3	2	0	0	1	2	3	5	5

The name of 'Chelsea' comes up frequently in the annals of Reading Football Club despite the infrequency of their meetings.

Ted Drake, as Manager, after five years at Elm Park took the club to the brink of promotion to the Second Division, then surprisingly resigned to take over at Stamford Bridge where he became one of the true all-time greats. He moulded youngsters at Chelsea, known as 'Drake's Ducklings', and in 1955 took the club to the League Championship, the first player/manager to do so. Equally famous was Chelsea's Roy Bentley, whom Reading tried in 1956 to coax to Elm Park. This move failed, but seven years later he arrived, as Manager, and stayed for seven seasons.

On the playing front, two personalities at Chelsea could well have become Reading players - Peter Bonetti and Peter Osgood, who in their youth came to training sessions run by Manager Harry Johnston, but both slipped through the net.

No doubt younger fans will be more likely look to the recent past and the two matches with the mega-millionaire London club in the Premiership. Despite their pedigree, in the 2006/07 season, the League Champions only managed a 1-0 victory at the Madejski Stadium (the start of an uncharacteristic run of five Reading defeats) and were held 2-2 in the return match.

Cheltenham Town

~ Playing Record ~

Competition	Played	Home					Away					Total	
(Total)		W	D	L	F	A	W	D	L	F	A	F	A
F.A.Cup	4	2	0	0	5	2	1	1	0	3	2	8	4

Although the Gloucestershire club have become a more or less established Football League club, having been promoted in 2000, the two teams have only met competitively in four matches, all in the F.A. Cup.

The first time was in the 1950/51 season when Reading predictably won the first round tie. Far more recently the two were drawn together in the 1996/97 season, and still a non-League side, Cheltenham held their First Division (second tier) opponents to a 1-1 draw before losing the third round match replay 2-1 at Elm Park.

Between times, the match at Whaddon Road on the 17th of November 1956, provides a statistic to go down in the record books, for on that day the first round tie drew an all-time record crowd of 8,326. The Robins had played at the ground since 1927, and it was one of the earliest in Britain, in 1950, to have floodlights.

Despite the enthusiasm of the local fans, who were supporting a successful team at this time, they couldn't lift the players sufficiently, and thanks to two goals from Tommy Dixon (one of five with this surname to have played for the club), Reading won 2-1 and went on to meet another non-League team, Bedford Town, in the second round.

Chester City

The

Biscuitmen

The first meeting between these two clubs was in the F.A.Cup (and subsequently to date the only time in that competition) during the 1935/36 season. Chester were relative newcomers to the Football League having only been elected in 1931, but when the two teams were drawn in the Cup's second round they were both fighting realistic chances of Championship wins - Reading in the Third Division South, and their rivals in the counterpart Northern section.

Dismissals by referees in this era were very rare, but Chester's half-back Howarth missed the Cup match through a sending-off and consequent suspension. Yet the North v. South Cup game was a very sociable affair, the hosts at Sealand Road presenting their opponents with a local Cheshire Cheese before the kick-off. Later, the homesters appeared to be coasting with a 3-1 lead, but Reading pulled two goals back to earn an Elm Park replay.

Returning the complement, Chester were presented with a tin of biscuits (Huntley and Palmers of course), and in the match were comfortably beaten 3-0.

A few weeks later Chester crushed York City 12-0 in a League match, but eventually only finished as runners-up in their division (ironically to their near namesake's 'Chesterfield'). Reading were similarly disappointed ending up third in their table.

Chesterfield

The

Biscuitmen

	~ Playing Record ~											
Competition	Played	Home					Away					Total	
	(Total)	W	D	L	F	A	W	D	L	F	A	F	A
League	30	5	5	5	23	19	3	2	10	18	35	41	54

Reading didn't encounter the Derbyshire side until the 1958/59 season, in the new Third Division (The Spireites having been in the Third Division North). The following season produced the most goals in a match between the clubs of those played in the League to date.

The home game was played on the 10th of October, and The Biscuitmen had made a poor start to the season, for after 14 games only two had been won. Chesterfield had made a modest start with four victories, although several games had been high-scoring, a 5-1 victory and the same result in reverse, and in just the previous match they triumphed 4-1, but all their 'away' matches had been defeats.

The first strike in the October game came direct from a Jimmy Wheeler corner, a rare enough event, then there was a flood of goals each side of half-time. In a playing period of just six minutes, four were added to the scoreline. But this was far from the end for the fans were to be treated to another four before the end of ninety minutes. Nine goals in this one match, and Reading claimed six of them.

Reading continued to improve as the season wore on, finishing mid-table at the end, whilst The Spireites struggled near the bottom.

Colchester United

~ Playing Record ~

Competition	Played (Total)	Home					Away					Total	
		W	D	L	F	A	W	D	L	F	A	F	A
League	52	16	4	6	53	28	6	7	13	42	51	95	79
F.A.Cup	6	2	1	0	10	3	2	0	1	7	5	17	8
League Cup	5	1	0	1	4	6	0	1	2	3	6	7	12

Whilst the two clubs have met on plenty of occasions in the Football League, from the 1950's up until the 21st century, it is a variety of circumstances which provide several memorable occasions.

The pair first met in 1946, when Reading thrashed their non-League opponents 5-0 in the F.A.Cup first round. Two years later the two met in the Cup again, this time Reading's visit encouraging the all-time record attendance at Layer Road, of 13,371; The Biscuitmen won 4-2. In 1954 the F.A.Cup match was played at Elm Park, and a series of events in the first half provided plenty of excitement. First the visitors raced into a two goal lead, then Reading had a brace of goals disallowed, before they finally scored a pair that were allowed to stand. The match eventually ended in a draw, and Reading won the replay.

In 1956, on February the 27th, it was the home League match that was to become literally the highlight when the club entertained Colchester in the first ever match in the competition under floodlights (a previously postponed fixture). In 1957, Reading beat Colchester 7-0 (their record defeat), and finally, by coincidence the Essex club were the first to 'christen' the new Elm Park floodlights in 1969.

Corinthians

The
Biscuitmen

~ *Playing Record* ~

Competition	Played	Home					Away					Total	
	(Total)	W	D	L	F	A	W	D	L	F	A	F	A
F.A.Cup	1	1	0	0	8	3	0	0	0	0	0	8	3

Apart from the club's very early days, when Reading came across occasional players from this world famous Amateur club, they only met once, on F.A.Cup duty.

The very name, 'The Corinthians', evokes the best of the Amateur game, a sporting and honest spirit. The club, formed in 1822, from the very best of footballers in the country, had written into their rules (number seven), that *"The Club shall not compete for any challenge cup or any prizes of any description whatsoever."* Initially they played top class Friendly matches, before relaxing their rule and entering for the F.A.Cup, initially in the 1922/23 season.

By the time Reading were drawn at home to this club in the first round of the 1935/36 competition, their visitors prowess had decreased, and The Biscuitmen comfortably thrashed their opponents 8-3. Yet the visitors were in total control for 30 minutes by which time they had taken a two goal lead. But the professionals began to make their mark, and by half-time they had levelled the score, then the tiring amateurs were outplayed in the second period. The final score has become Reading's biggest in the proper rounds of the competition, The Corinthians worst defeat, and the attendance of 15,998 was the largest of the round.

Coventry City

The

Biscuitmen

~ Playing Record ~

Competition	Played (Total)	Home					Away					Total	
		W	D	L	F	A	W	D	L	F	A	F	A
League	40	13	4	3	43	22	3	6	11	16	33	59	55
F.A.Cup	3	0	1	0	2	2	$1	1	0	4	3	6	5

From 1925, and for many years in the Third Division South, the two clubs met. During this period there was an intriguing run of four matches in a period of just ten days in December 1932.

The first of this series, on the 3rd, was a run-of-the-mill League game at Elm Park which ended in a 3-3 draw, The Biscuitmen having made an excellent start to the season, losing only two of their Third Division games up to Christmas. One week later Coventry were again the visitors, this time for an F.A.Cup first round match which was also drawn, this time four goals were shared. Such was the power of the Cup at this time, that the attendance of over 13,000 was nearly double that of a week earlier.

Five days later (unusually on a Thursday afternoon - presumably half-day closing in Coventry) the two teams met again, at Highfield Road, and a 3-3 draw was the outcome. This result required the tie to go to a second replay, when at this time such matches were played on a neutral ground. On the 19th of December, a sparse crowd of 6,676 at Stamford Bridge, were present to witness Reading at last break the deadlock with a single goal win.

Chelsea's Frank Lampard scores the only goal at Reading.

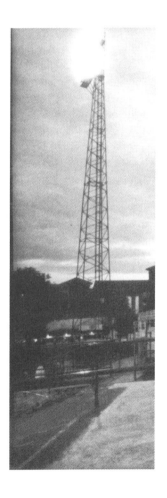

(Above)
Dunphy scored one of the five
goals against Crewe Alexandra.
(Left)
The new floodlights made their
'debut' versus Colchester United.

(Above)
Edelston, seen here, scoring one of the goals when Crystal Palace were beaten 10-2.

(Left)
Maurice Evans, who became the stand-in Goalkeeper during the Enfield F.A.Cup match.

Derby County were beaten 5-0, and Long scored one of the goals.

Crewe Alexandra

~ Playing Record ~

Competition	Played	Home					Away					Total	
	(Total)	W	D	L	F	A	W	D	L	F	A	F	A
League	32	10	6	0	35	12	3	7	6	18	21	53	33

The club from the railway town featured twice, albeit both times having no direct effect, in Reading's history during the 1970's.

The first was for the very last match of the 1975/76 season, when Crewe were entertained at Elm Park. Having already secured promotion from the Fourth Division, there was no pressure on the team, and the supporters turned out in force, the attendance of 12,440 being the second highest of the season. Three goals coming from the ill-fated Robin Friday, Eamonn Dunphy (one of only three scored for the club) and Dennis Nelson. The latter, was an ex-Alex. player having arrived at Elm Park in March 1975 for a £10,000 fee, and ironically two years later he made the return journey to Gresty Road on a free transfer.

In the close season of 1979, Hughie Cheetham was signed from Crewe Alexandra, the fee of £25,000 being a record sum for Reading. 21-year-old Cheetham was a product of Crewe's youth policy which has produced many players who have moved on to greater fame; but not Hughie. After a handful of games he lost his place in the first team, returned for one match a few weeks later - when he broke a bone in his foot - and in 1981 he drifted into non-League football.

Crystal Palace

Competition	Played (Total)	Home					Away					Total	
		W	D	L	F	A	W	D	L	F	A	F	A
League	66	17	7	9	69	42	10	11	12	45	50	114	92
F.A.Cup	6	0	1	2	2	5	0	2	$1	2	4	4	9

~ Playing Record ~

With over 60 games to chose from, there could arguably be a number that are worth highlighting, but most Reading fans will agree that - despite it occurring over 60 years ago - there is one match that grabs centre stage.

The 1946/47 season was the first full campaign return to normal football after the war. The fixture list for the ill-fated 1939/40 season was repeated, and therefore Reading's first home match was versus Crystal Palace, whom they had beaten 5-0 in their one of three matches played before the hostilities. But the result following the meeting on the 4th of September 1946, dwarfed all others.

With two debutants in the team in Maurice Edelston (son of manager Joe) and newcomer Vic Barney - both of whom became goalscorers in the match - the team went on the rampage. It was 1-0 after just four minutes and two more were scored after fifteen, yet by half-time Palace had pulled back two goals; half-time 3-2 to Reading. After 47 minutes a two goal lead was restored, from the penalty spot, and from then on there was no stopping The Biscuitmen. The top marksmen was 'Tony' McPhee with four, and Edelston with a debut hat-trick. The final tally was 10-2 to Reading, the Club's all-time record score.

Dagenham

The

Biscuitmen

~ Playing Record ~

Competition	Played	Home					Away					Total	
	(Total)	W	D	L	F	A	W	D	L	F	A	F	A
F.A.Cup	2	0	1	0	1	1	1	0	0	1	0	2	1

Not to be confused with the current club 'Dagenham and Redbridge' formerly of the Vauxhall Conference and at the time of writing just promoted to the Football League, 'this' Dagenham was an earlier version. There was a pre-war club with the same name, then another founded in 1949, before a series of takeovers and renaming which involved four different clubs in East London, leading eventually to the current incarnation in 1992.

In the 1967/68 season, Reading were drawn at home to play 'Dagenham F.C.' in the second round of the F.A.Cup. At this time this club was a modest, but, at their level, successful Amateur club playing in the Athenian League (in which they became Champions that season). Therefore what should have been an easy task for Reading, became an uphill struggle. The visitors to Elm Park displayed a determined style, and were far more robust than their Amateur status suggested. Before a stunned crowd of over 12,000, Dagenham led their professional opponents, and only a late equaliser from winger George Harris saved the home team's blushes.

The replay, before a packed 8,000 Victoria Road Ground, produced more of the same, and a somewhat fortuitous - disputed - goal from John Sainty saw Reading through to the third round.

Darlington

The **Biscuitmen**

~ Playing Record ~

Competition	Played (Total)	Home					Away					Total	
		W	D	L	F	A	W	D	L	F	A	F	A
League	24	10	1	1	23	8	6	2	4	15	13	38	21
F.A.Cup	1	0	0	1	0	1	0	0	0	0	0	0	1
League Cup	1	0	>1	0	3	3	0	0	0	0	0	3	3

Although the two clubs have not met on many occasions, there are three which stand out as having had a great significance in the history of Reading F.C., and indeed football itself.

The first meeting was back in the 1924/25 season, in an F.A.Cup match. Until this time a foul throw was punished with a free kick to the opposition, something that clubs, and Reading in particular had complained about. In this match The Biscuitmen lost the game to Darlington by the only goal of the game through such an incident. Ironically, from the next season onwards the F.A. agreed, and the result of the infringement was replaced, which remains to this day, with a throw-in to the opposition. Incidentally, the attendance of 17,203 was, at that time a record for an F.A.Cup-tie at Elm Park.

In the 1971/72 season, when Steve Hetzke ran out at Feethams, Darlington, on December the 18th, he became, at 16 years and 193 days, the all-time youngest player to represent Reading in a competitive match; his presence however, couldn't prevent a single goal defeat. Fifteen years later the result of the same fixture on the 19th April was a different story, for the goalless draw ensured The Royals were promoted to the Second Division.

Dartford

The
Biscuitmen

Over the years many non-League clubs have been encountered in the F.A.Cup and in the 1950/51 season two such teams were the opponents. Dartford, the only time the clubs met, were entertained at Elm Park, after Cheltenham had been beaten in the first round.

The Southern League team were doughty F.A.Cup fighters, this being the tenth time they had reached the 'proper' rounds since 1927, their best performances coming in 1936 when they only lost by 3-2 to Derby County in the third round. In 1950, the visitors were somewhat struggling in the Southern League, whilst Reading were holding their own in the Third, albeit a better second half of the season saw them finish third in the table. Therefore if the Cup match went to plan, Reading should win comfortably - which they did!

Goals from former Schoolboy International Les Henley, Maurice Edelston (son of former manager, Joe), Ron Blackman (arguably Reading's best ever centre-forward) and Ken Bainbridge (his second that season in the Cup, of only three in total) produced a 4-0 victory, before a crowd numbering 17,185.

Sadly, 'this' Dartford became defunct in 1992, when they became joint victims (the other being groundsharers Maidstone United, short term members of the Fourth Division) when their ground at Watling Street was sold for development.

Derby County

~ Playing Record ~

Competition	Played (Total)	Home					Away					Total	
		W	D	L	F	A	W	D	L	F	A	F	A
League	18	7	1	1	17	5	2	2	5	10	21	27	26
League Cup	4	2	0	0	5	1	0	1	1	1	3	6	4

Despite not having played The Rams in that many League games, several have been significant. Notably in the mid-1980's, the home match near the end of the 1985/86 season was deemed the Championship decider, and one goal from Trevor Senior gave The Royals the three points, and indeed virtually assured them of the Third Division title.

A year later, and a last home game win over Derby County this time was necessary to guarantee continued Second Division football at Elm Park. Trevor Senior again obliged, this time with a brace of goals.

Perhaps the most significant match (and the most recent) against this team was that in the 2005/06 season. Once again it was a 'decider', for a home victory over The Rams on the 1st of April, would confirm The Championship title, even with four more matches still to play. The Royals were certainly no fools, for they made no mistake about the result. Despite a quiet first half, the second was in complete contrast, with five goals in the space of 24 minutes which completely overwhelmed the visitors. Although not the end of the season, it crowned a glorious campaign, and a move up to join the cream of football in England.

Doncaster Rovers

The

Biscuitmen

Competition	Played (Total)	Home					Away					Total	
		W	D	L	F	A	W	D	L	F	A	F	A
League	32	13	1	2	36	11	8	6	2	33	22	69	33
F.A.Cup	2	1	0	1	4	3	0	0	0	0	0	4	3

~ Playing Record ~

The 1958/59 season saw a re-arrangement in the lower divisions, the bottom halves of the former North and South Divisions forming the new 'Fourth Division' and the top halves, the new 'Third.' Reading, by finishing fifth in their table earned their place, but it was relegation from the Second that required Rovers to visit Elm Park on the 6th of September.

Doncaster were the first visitors from the North, Reading having already drawn with Q.P.R. and comfortably beaten Southend United. A modest start to the season was improved upon with a 2-0 victory, Jimmy Whitehouse and Sylvan Anderton being the marksmen. But who amongst the spectators present would have believed that they had just seen a T.V. star of the future in action for the visitors? Centre-half Charlie Williams (later M.B.E.), unusual for this period, a black player, was a near ever-present for Donny the previous two seasons, having joined them in 1956, and he stayed at Belle Vue before pursuing a stage career, as a stand-up comedian and in particular as host of Television's 'Golden Shot.' Barnsley-born, he made 171 appearances for Rovers, his only club. As a centre-half, he said that he.... *"was never a fancy player, but could stop the players that were!"*

Enfield

The

Biscuitmen

~ Playing Record ~

Competition	Played (Total)	Home					Away					Total	
		W	D	L	F	A	W	D	L	F	A	F	A
F.A.Cup	2	0	1	0	2	2	1	0	0	4	2	6	4

Reading made little progress in the F.A.Cup in the 1963/64 season, losing in the second round at fellow Third Division club, and strugglers, Luton Town, yet it was a close thing that they even got that far!

Enfield, were newly promoted to the Isthmian League (the most senior Amateur competition in the South), but Reading should have nonetheless had little trouble in disposing of the club from North London, at Elm Park. Yet it was the visitors who had taken a commanding two goal lead, before goals from Jimmy Wheeler and Denis Allen saved the professionals' blushes.

In the replay at Southbury Road, before a near 7,500 crowd, it looked like plain sailing when this time Reading took a two goal lead. Yet the Amateurs fought back and after 90 minutes the score was 2-2. Although Reading scored twice in injury time, it could have been a different story, for goalkeeper Arthur Wilkie was injured early into the 30 minutes, and only the inspired performance of his stand-in Maurice Evans, kept the Enfield forwards at bay. Wilkie was also injured four years earlier in a match against Halifax, but played on out wide on the wing, and amazingly scored two goals, the only time this has happened in Football League history.

Erith & Belvedere

The
Biscuitmen

Competition	Played (Total)	Home					Away					Total	
		W	D	L	F	A	W	D	L	F	A	F	A
F.A.Cup	1	0	0	0	0	0	1	0	0	2	0	2	0

~ *Playing Record* ~

There is little to relate to between this side from Kent and The Royals. Just one meeting in the F.A.Cup, and two players who on leaving Elm Park, finished their careers at the non-League club.

The sole meeting was in 1924/25, the season having commenced in a fairly mundane fashion for Reading, and by mid-November they lay midway in the Third Division South table. Just a few months earlier, the Kent League Amateurs had completed a most successful season, having reached the F.A. Amateur Cup Final. In this run they had beaten the renowned London Caledonians after a second replay. 'The Deres' had only been formed in 1922, from an earlier club created four years earlier. A crowd of around 3,000 were present at their compact Park View ground (which sadly in the recent past they have had to vacate), most in the hope that the underdog amateurs could beat the visiting professionals.

But the match went more or less to form, with two goals from Reading's William Fergusson sealing a victory. Fergusson, who had been signed from Oldham earlier in 1924, never really made it with Reading and left at the end of the season.

The two players, both in the 1980's, that moved on, were Paul Canoville and loanee Micky Nutton.

Everton

~ Playing Record ~

Competition	Played	Home					Away					Total	
	(Total)	W	D	L	F	A	W	D	L	F	A	F	A
League	4	0	0	2	0	4	0	1	1	3	4	3	8
League Cup	1	0	0	0	0	0	0	0	1	0	1	0	1

There was 75 years before the first League meetings between the two and the next. And the four games provide a somewhat grim statistic, the Merseyside team being one of the very few never beaten by The Royals.

The 1930/31 season was in itself a disastrous one, Reading having survived the previous four years in Division Two, this campaign was to prove even worse. When the pair met in November, Reading had won just two of their 12 League games to that point. In contrast Everton were riding high, and a 2-0 Elm Park defeat that day, and a 3-2 reverse the following March in the return were hardly surprises. The Toffees finished as Champions and The Biscuitment - at second from bottom - were relegated.

The results of the two encounters in the 2006/07 season were not a lot better, although the circumstances certainly were. A bright start to the Premiership saw The Royals holding seventh in the table whilst the visitors were just behind, two days before Christmas. But a 2-1 Reading defeat saw these positions reversed. In the return in mid-January, a fortuitous own goal in the first half looked as if Reading might on this occasion win, before a goalkeeping error allowed the home team to equalise in the 81st minute.

Exeter City

~ Playing Record ~

Competition	Played (Total)	Home					Away					Total	
		W	D	L	F	A	W	D	L	F	A	F	A
League	82	31	6	4	89	35	16	7	18	67	76	156	111
* F.A.Cup													

With so much involvement and games played with The Grecians over the years it is difficult to pick just one memorable or outstanding event.

For humour (although not at the time) it could be in the goalless draw at Elm Park in 1922, when the visiting player (captain) Kirk swallowed his false teeth and only salty water allowed him to regurgitate them..... For sadness it has be the death of former manager (of both clubs) Arthur Chadwick who soon after his retirement died in 1931 whilst watching a match at St. James' Park.

For the spectacular, the home match against Exeter in the 1973/74 season takes pride of place. This saw the home debut of Friday, on a Sunday, instead of Saturday. This was the first Sunday match staged in Reading (due to the Countrywide power crisis) and will always be remembered by the fans as the 'arrival' of Robin Friday. The irrepressible centre-forward scored two spectacular goals in his team's 4-1 victory.... Finally for despair one could look to the 1981/82 season, when Exeter City were beaten 4-0 in late March which lifted the team to second in the League, yet the attendance had been a pathetic 3,601; a dismal run-in saw the team finally finish mid-table, but the average League attendance that season was a dismal 4,026.

Fulham

The

Biscuitmen

~ Playing Record ~

Competition	Played (Total)	Home					Away					Total	
		W	D	L	F	A	W	D	L	F	A	F	A
League	30	8	2	5	18	17	4	5	6	17	20	35	37
* F.A.Cup	1	0	0	1	1	2	0	0	0	0	0	1	2
League Cup	5	0	2	1	2	3	1	1	0	4	2	6	5

Frank Newton was a prolific goalscorer with Fulham during the early 1930's (as he was at his previous club Stockport County). In the 1931/ 32 season, 'Bonzo' as he was known netted 43 League goals, an all-time Fulham record. Next season he added goals in nine consecutive matches, before asking for a move in the Autumn of 1933, to Reading, citing his wife's request to move away from London, which was granted; quite amazing since at this time The Cottagers, in Division Two, were one division higher than Reading and the fee of £650 was very little for such an established striker.

The Fulham board were so incensed that their manager, James McIntyre (ironically a former Reading player) was immediately sacked for taking the decision upon himself. Yet this wasn't the end of the story, for despite continuing his rich vein of goalscoring, Newton moved back to Fulham in October 1934.

Controversy reared its head again, when Reading Director William Lee indiscreetly informed the Press that after the club's 1-0 defeat at Watford, he stated that the match had been a *"disgracefully weak exhibition and Newton was the worst centre-forward ever seen in the Third Division."* A ludicrous statement about a player that had netted 31 goals in 34 games!

Everton scored an 'own goal' at Goodison Park, and Ingimarsson was in attendance.

Arthur Chadwick managed both
Reading and Exeter City.

Frank Newton was involved in controversial moves between Fulham and Reading.

Three members of the team for the first ever Football League match at Elm Park, against Gillingham: Bailey, Andrews and 'keeper Crawford.

Webb (far right) and Shreeves....

...the goalscorers in the Halifax Town match.

Prolific goalscorer, Senior, who achieved a new Reading record against Hartlepool United.

Gillingham

The Biscuitmen

~ Playing Record ~

Competition	Played	Home					Away					Total	
	(Total)	W	D	L	F	A	W	D	L	F	A	F	A
League	88	25	7	12	83	47	9	11	24	42	75	125	122
F.A.Cup	6	2	1	0	8	4	2	1	0	5	3	13	7
League Cup	7	2	0	1	6	2	2	1	1	4	6	10	8

Although there is a large selection to choose from, one of the most significant matches was the meeting of the two teams for the first time in the Football League in the 1920/21 season, which was also The Biscuitmen's first home game in the new Third Division.

The team had already got off to a good start by winning 1-0 at Newport County. In these pre-floodlit days, the kick-off for the Wednesday evening fixture was at 6.00 p.m., and just one minute later the first Elm Park Football League goal was scored - by the opposition. Worse was to follow, for the same player, Tom Gilbey, added a second goal, before Reading's Bert Yarnell reduced the arrears soon after. Ironically this was Yarnell's first and only goal for the club, within just five appearances; an injury later in September kept him on the sidelines and he never re-appeared in the first team. Offside and time wasting tactics in the second half prevented an equaliser, but some extra entertainment was appreciated by the spectators when a powerful shot from George Getgood became a direct hit on the referee!

The attendance for this 'opener' was a surprisingly poor 7,000 or so, and in fact the club's baptism eventually produced the lowest average in the whole Football League that season, of 7,150.

Grays Athletic

~ Playing Record ~

Competition	Played	Home					Away					Total	
	(Total)	W	D	L	F	A	W	D	L	F	A	F	A
F.A.Cup	1	1	0	0	4	0	0	0	0	0	0	4	0

In the 1949/50 season, Ray Kemp, a young amateur goalkeeper with this Essex amateur club was signed during an injury emergency period, and was on the winning side twice in his three games.

Fifty years later, in the F.A.Cup at the Madejeski Stadium, the complete Grays Athletic team did not fare so well. The Ryman League visitors hardly arrived in confident mood, having that season not recorded an away victory, whilst Reading were riding high in the Football League Division Two. Although outplayed, the visitors lacked nothing in effort, and the atmosphere that afternoon was generated by their 500 or so fans. In fact one could almost have been forgiven for thinking that The Royals were on to a defeat, for the poor crowd numbering only 5,643 remained almost silent throughout. Yet it was Reading who scored the goals, all four, without reply. A half-time lead, from Lee Hodges, was added to in the second period from Jamie Cureton, Martin Butler and a late Keith Jones strike in the 87th minute.

Grays finished 15th of 22 clubs in their League, whilst Reading stormed on to the Play-off Final. But the fortunes for both have improved since, with the Essex team currently a member of the Conference.

Grimsby Town

The

Biscuitmen

Competition	Played (Total)	Home					Away					Total	
		W	D	L	F	A	W	D	L	F	A	F	A
League	44	9	7	6	40	24	5	5	12	21	39	61	63
F.A.Cup	5	1	1	1	7	4	0	1	1	2	4	9	8

~ Playing Record ~

With The Royals, at the time of writing, worthy members of the Premiership, and The Mariners languishing in the Football League Second Division, the roles were reversed at the F.A.Cup meeting in the 1946/47 season. Even so, before an Elm Park crowd of 22,890, modest Third Division club Reading held their First Division opponents to a third round 2-2 draw, earned by virtue of a tremendous comeback from being two goals down after only six minutes. But the replay was too much and they lost 3-1.

Twenty years later, Reading had started their Third Division campaign in dismal fashion, recording just three victories in their opening 17 League fixtures, when they had failed to score in six of these. Grimsby were the visitors on the 16th of November 1966, and The Biscuitmen were on the end of a run of seven matches without a victory. But against this form the team went on to win 6-0, equalling their total number of goals scored in the previous seven games.

From then on it was an upward surge to the end. An average of two goals a game, and only one when they didn't score. But it wasn't quite enough for they finished fourth in the table, just two points below promoted Middlesborough in second place.

Guildford City

The
Biscuitmen

~ Playing Record ~

Competition	Played	Home					Away					Total	
	(Total)	W	D	L	F	A	W	D	L	F	A	F	A
F.A.Cup	1	0	0	0	0	0	0	0	1	0	1	0	1

In their long history, Reading only met Guildford City once in a competitive match. And in view of the result they probably wish the meeting had never happened!

The Biscuitmen had only made a modest start to the season and by the time of the first round of the F.A.Cup in November 1937 they lay around mid-table in the Third Division South. Meanwhile, Guildford City were enjoying one of their most successful periods, being reigning Southern League Champions, and well on the way to a second title (in fact they finished runners-up that season to Colchester United). In the circumstances, perhaps the final result was not such a surprise. This was the sixth time that the Joseph's Road club had reached this stage in the Cup, and there was a record attendance of 7,831 (paying £450 total receipts).

Guildford pulled of a surprise, scoring the only goal after 30 minutes, but one newspaper report hardly congratulated them: "*In quite the poorest, scrappiest and most dismal game I have seen this season, Reading took their knockout blow in the F.A.Cup at Guildford this afternoon.*" This was Reading's first dismissal in the competition to a non-League side, but at least they picked up League form during the rest of the season and finished sixth in the final table.

Halifax Town

Competition	Played	Home					Away					Total	
~ *Playing Record* ~													
	(Total)	W	D	L	F	A	W	D	L	F	A	F	A
League	20	7	3	0	21	9	3	3	4	12	17	33	26
F.A.Cup	2	0	1	0	1	1	1	0	0	1	0	2	1

Although meetings against the Yorkshire team have been fairly rare, there are three matches involving them that stand out.

In the 1958/59 season, after Tommy Dixon had been sold to Brighton for £4,250, Willie Gardiner was signed from Blackpool, hopefully to take over the mantle as a reliable goalscorer. Ironically he was unsuccessful in his first game, a 3-0 home win over Halifax in November, yet scored in his next two games (both defeats). These became his only goals for the club as he sustained a leg injury soon after that effectively ended his playing career.

Four seasons later, briefly mentioned elsewhere, goalkeeper Arthur Wilkie was the goalscoring hero in Reading's 4-2 home victory over the Shaymen. Injured, he left the field in the first half, returned in the second (no substitutes then), and from playing on the wing netted a brace of goals; the only 'Keeper ever to score two goals in a League game.

Later that season, on the 11th of May, Reading looked doomed for a drop to the Fourth Division, and that day travelled to play already relegated Halifax. Before a crowd of just 1,202 (one of the lowest to watch a League match involving Reading), goals from Dougie Webb and Peter Shreeves in a 2-1 win ensured their survival (the last two games were lost!)

Hartlepool United

The Biscuitmen

Competition	Played (Total)	Home					Away					Total	
		W	D	L	F	A	W	D	L	F	A	F	A
League	24	8	2	2	29	7	5	3	4	21	20	50	27

~ Playing Record ~

Of the 24 Football League games against The 'Pool, two, significantly involved goalscoring.

It was obvious at the start of the 1968/69 season that a goalscorer was needed (just four goals in five games). Former Reading junior, Peter Silvester, had been an irregular member of the first team for three seasons, came on as a substitute at Swindon, a scoreless draw, and with Roger Smee out with a broken ankle was given a starting chance at home against Hartlepool. In spectacular fashion, he scored four goals in The Biscuitmen's seven-nil demolition of a Hartlepool side that was destined to struggle for the rest of the season. Silvester was a virtual ever-present for the rest of the season and added another eight goals to his League tally.

The final game of the 1983/84 season was played at Hartlepool United. The result was academic since The Royals had already earned their promotion back into the Third Division at the first attempt. But for Trevor Senior the match had particular significance, and the 700 or so travelling fans celebrated with him when he netted a brace of goals in the 3-3 draw. This took his total to 41 for the season, a new all-time Reading goalscoring record, and also made him the top marksman in the country that season.

Hayes

~ *Playing Record* ~

Competition	Played	Home					Away					Total	
	(Total)	W	D	L	F	A	W	D	L	F	A	F	A
F.A.Cup	2	0	1	0	0	0	0	1	0	0	1	0	1	0

There have been several players that have been involved with both clubs, although since Hayes, in West Middlesex, is relatively close to Reading, perhaps these inter-player movements are not surprising.

The one that stands out above all others was Robin Friday. Friday came to Reading's notice when he played against them in the two 1972/73 F.A.Cup-ties, a somewhat embarrassing scoreless draw at home and a marginal one goal victory at Church Road. He came to Reading on trial, starred in the reserves, signed permanently and then made the first team after two impressive displays away from Elm Park in early 1974.

Michael Meaker was a local Hayes man, born in nearby Greenford, who signed for Reading from Q.P.R. in a half million pound deal in the 1995 close season. A frustrating player who never quite made it at Reading, he does hold the distinction of scoring the last ever League goal at Elm Park. Gary Westwood was snapped up by The Royals, after an impressive trial period, from Ipswich. Despite hailing from the North-west, one of his non-League clubs at the end of his playing career was Hayes.

James Quinn in the early nineteen-nineties hardly needs any introduction, and amongst his myriad of clubs, Hayes was one, where he acted in a Managerial role.

Hendon

The Biscuitmen

Competition	Played (Total)	Home					Away					Total	
		W	D	L	F	A	W	D	L	F	A	F	A
F.A.Cup	3	1	0	0	4	2	1	0	1	3	2	7	4

~ *Playing Record* ~

It may comes as a surprise to many Royals' fans that their team have met Hendon on five occasions in the F.A.Cup. Albeit the meetings in the 1878/79 season (a 1-0 victory which took the team on to play the renowned and former finalists Old Etonians) and again three seasons later when the Middlesex side were swept aside 5-0, were against a forerunner, with the same name, as the current non-League club.

In 1967, eighty-five years later, the two teams met, and Reading had little trouble winning 3-1 at Claremont Road before a crowd numbering 4,050. Two of the goals were scored by Rod Thornhill, a local Amateur player snapped up by the club, who went on to make over 200 appearances for the club. However, 'Spider', as he was known, scored a total of only three goals in the F.A.Cup. In the 1975/76 season, an embarrassing return was made to North London, for the Fourth Division team made headlines of the wrong type when they lost by a single goal.

This defeat was forgotten by the season's end for the team finished third in the table and were promoted. Finally, the 1988/89 season saw Hendon as visitors to Elm Park, but there were no surprises, the homesters winning 4-2.

Hereford United

~ Playing Record ~

Competition	Played (Total)	Home					Away					Total	
		W	D	L	F	A	W	D	L	F	A	F	A
League	6	2	0	1	6	2	0	2	1	1	4	7	6
F.A.Cup	3	2	0	0	4	0	0	0	1	0	1	4	1

The club's meetings with this West country team have been few, but the most notable was in the second Fourth Division game of the 1972/73 season.

On the strength of their strong displays in the Southern League (although they only finished runners-up in 1972), plus their much publicised F.A.Cup run that season which included the beating of the mighty Newcastle United at Edgar Street, Hereford were elected to the Football League for the 1972/73 season. This caused some controversy, and anguish, as their election was at the expense of Barrow, and only on a second vote.

The Bulls started their League career in disappointing fashion, losing 1-0 at Colchester, whilst Reading could only draw 1-1 at home to Crewe (amazingly, that season, one of only seven goals conceded at home in the League). But The Bulls' first home game, on the 19th of August, produced an enormous, 8,839 crowd in their compact enclosure. It was bad luck for Reading that they were the opponents that day, as carrying on the air of euphoria, The Biscuitmen were subdued by The Bulls, with a 3-0 scoreline. Hereford completed the double over Reading that season, and went on to finish second in the table and hence were promoted to the Third Division, thereby fully justifying their position with the 'elite'.

Huddersfield Town

Competition	Played	Home					Away					Total	
	(Total)	W	D	L	F	A	W	D	L	F	A	F	A
League	36	11	4	3	28	17	7	3	8	20	27	48	44
F.A.Cup	2	1	0	0	2	1	0	1	0	0	0	2	1
League Cup	1	1	0	0	1	0	0	0	0	0	0	1	0

~ Playing Record ~

The quirkiest incident featuring Huddersfield Town and Reading occurred late in the 1988/89 season and involved a missed penalty.

Aside from 'real' football, Elm Park was also host to a struggling Second Division team led by a female football manager aka Gabriella Benson (actress Cherie Lunghi)! This was for the TV series entitled 'The Manageress'. For promotion, 'her' team were required to win their last match ('played' at Elm Park). They were leading 1-0, when a penalty was awarded to the 'visitors'. The teams consisted of professional actors plus mostly Reading reserve and youth players. The drama required that the penalty, taken by penalty expert Stuart Beavon, be saved. Equally it had to be convincing, and it required ten attempts before the 'save' met with the approval of the Director (Christopher King).

Two weeks later, on the 7th of March, Beavon was called upon to take a real penalty (that season he had already converted three) in the Huddersfield Town match at Leeds Road. He missed, citing the excuse that he had now become accustomed to not scoring, having been instructed to miss them earlier! Reading drew the match 2-2, but Beavon redeemed himself with four more successful spot kicks before the end of that season.

Hull City

The
Biscuitmen

~ Playing Record ~

Competition	Played	Home					Away					Total	
	(Total)	W	D	L	F	A	W	D	L	F	A	F	A
League	40	9	6	5	34	20	7	7	6	20	23	54	43
* F.A.Cup	2	0	0	1	1	2	0	1	0	0	0	1	2

The two clubs have met each other on League duty in 40 matches to date (although only twice in one of the two major cup competitions), which have embraced most decades over the last near ninety years. Interestingly Reading have been called upon to visit four different Hull City 'home' grounds in all.

The first meeting - although prior to the period generally covered here - was an F.A.Cup match in the 1905/06 season. This finished as a surprise 1-0 Reading victory over the Second Division club, which was played at The Circle Ground, in fact the Cricket Ground, in Anlaby Road (some of their League matches that season were played at The Boulevard, a rugby ground).

When the teams met in the Second Division in the 1920's, Hull's home was the Anlaby Road Football Ground, this venue lay immediately adjacent to the Cricket Ground. The next meeting was in the F.A.Cup during the 1948/49 season, when the match was staged at Boothferry Park, the football ground having been built in the early post-Second World War days.

Hull City"s final move, to the Kingston Communications Stadium in late 2002, last saw the two clubs fight out a 1-1 draw in October 2005, on The Royals' march to The Premiership.

Ilford

The
Biscuitmen

The two clubs in fact first met during the first Southern League season of 1894/95, and the following campaign saw the Essex side lose every game, their best result being a 3-1 defeat at Reading!

It was nearly forty years before the two clubs met again in their only other encounter. Inevitably this match was in the F.A. Cup, during the 1936/37 season. A 7,800 crowd packed into the compact but well appointed Lynn Road ground and the homesters stunned The Biscuitmen after taking a two goal lead. However the visitors fought back and had levelled the score by half-time. In the second period the amateurs conceded two more goals, and so Reading came away with a 4-2 victory.

In the second round, Reading thrashed Newport County 7-2, before narrowly losing by a single goal at Old Trafford, to a struggling First Division Manchester United side that were relegated that season.

Ilford F.C. were a much respected club that lost their identity in 1979 when they were forced to move out of their ground. They merged with Leytonstone, who in turn embraced Walthamstow Avenue, then Dagenham - in a series of East London mergers and takeovers. However, there is now another 'Ilford F.C.' who currently play in the Ryman League.

(Above) Taylor is on target in the Hendon Cup victory.

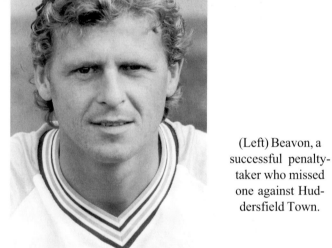

(Left) Beavon, a successful penalty-taker who missed one against Huddersfield Town.

A cartoon of the time relating to the Ilford F.A.Cup match.

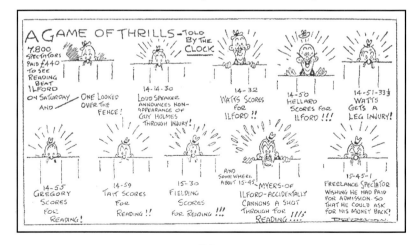

(Above) Mark McGhee, in his Reading playing days, who turned his back on The Royals in favour of Leicester City.

(Left) 'Bomber' Reeves scored from the penalty spot at Kings Lynn.

Said to be three years older than Reading, Leyton F.C. have been met in the F.A.Cup just once.

Ipswich Town

~ Playing Record ~

Competition	Played	Home					Away					Total	
	(Total)	W	D	L	F	A	W	D	L	F	A	F	A
League	40	9	4	7	32	34	5	4	11	27	37	59	71
* F.A.Cup	1	0	0	0	0	0	0	0	1	1	4	1	4

To many readers, it may come as a surprise that, although Ipswich didn't join the Football League until 1938, the two clubs first competed in the same competition, way back in the mists of time. The occasion was the 1893/94 season, the first of the F.A.Amateur Cup, and Reading's first of two entries.

The two clubs also met 112 years later, during the 2005/06 Football League Championship winning season, and the situation was somewhat different. On the 16th of October, The Royals were well into their amazing record-breaking run, and even the attendance of the Sky TV cameras at the Madjeski Stadium couldn't stop them from putting on another excellent display. They dominated the play, from the start outplaying the visitors, and the 2-0 scoreline was hardly a true reflection of the difference. It was an own goal, and one from Kevin Doyle that won the points.

Just a few weeks later, the return at Portman Road produced more of the same. Although this time the score of 3-0 to The Royals was more realistic. The goals came from Steve Sidwell, Leroy Lita and another from Doyle. This marked the team's 22nd consecutive game without defeat, their fourth win on the bounce, and their move to the top of the table.

Kettering Town

The

Biscuitmen

For most of their long history, the Northamptonshire club, The Poppies, have played in the Southern League. The two clubs first crossed swords in Reading's pre-Football League days, and when the Southern League was extended to 18, in 1903, Kettering and Wellingborough were the only clubs to not subsequently become Football League members.

Since 1920, the two teams have only met twice, both 4-2 victories in the F.A.Cup, in 1960 and 1979. The 1960/61 season saw The Biscuitmen struggling both financially and on the playing front in the Third Division. A Cup run, as well as a diversion it was hoped would help balance the books, and a 6-2 win at home to Millwall was a good start.

In the second round, Kettering were entertained, and a crowd of over 12,000 saw a relatively easy 4-2 victory. Yet the Poppies were not expected to be an easy walkover, for they were, around this time, one of the leading Southern League clubs, and seeking entry to the Football League.

In the third round, Reading could only draw with Barnsley, then lose the replay. Their fellow Third Division opponents went on a run to a replayed 6th round match, leaving Reading to only dream of the financial benefits such a run could have been to them!

Kings Lynn

The

Biscuitmen

~ *Playing Record* ~

Competition	Played	Home					Away					Total	
	(Total)	W	D	L	F	A	W	D	L	F	A	F	A
F.A.Cup	1	1	0	0	4	2	0	0	0	0	0	4	2

The club's only game against the East Anglian side was in the F.A.Cup during the 1959/60 season, and coincidentally the situation was very similar to the previous, alphabetical entry of 'Kettering Town'.

The season had started in horrendous fashion, and after eight games and just one point, the team were rooted at the bottom of the Third Division table. Fortunately an improved run saw a recovery and after beating Norwich City in the F.A.Cup first round, in a replay, Reading were drawn to play the non-Leaguers in the next tie. After a long and unremarkable record in the competition (Kings Lynn first entered in 1900) this was only the second time they had reached this stage (they then went on to make it five seasons in a row). Reading were not the draw that The Linnets wanted, for they would have preferred a far more lucrative local derby against Norwich City!

The coincidence with Kettering goes even further, for not only were Kings Lynn a moderately successful Southern League side, but the result on the 5th of December was the same - a 4-2 victory to the Biscuitmen. The Reading goalscorers were Bobby Ayre with a brace (his only F.A.Cup goals for the club), Ray 'Bomber' Reeves (a penalty) and Jimmy Wheeler.

Leeds United

~ Playing Record ~

Competition	Played	Home					Away					Total	
	(Total)	W	D	L	F	A	W	D	L	F	A	F	A
League	10	1	2	2	4	5	0	2	3	6	13	10	18
League Cup	2	0	0	0	0	0	0	1	0	1	4	4	4

Matches against the Yorkshire club have been few and far between, yet the fortunes of both clubs have changed dramatically since the second time the pair met in the League Cup.

The 1997/98 season finished with The Royals unable to hold on to their First Division (second tier) status, whilst Leeds United finished their season fifth from top in the premiership. On the 18th of November, Reading fifth from bottom in their division) were entertained at Elland Road, in the 4th round of the Coca-Cola (League Cup).

On paper The Royals stood little chance and their only win of note in the competition that season had been the 4-2 victory over fellow First Division club Wolves in the previous round. Yet in a surprisingly poorly attended match (little over 15,000), Reading took a ninth minute lead through Carl Asaba, although the elation did not last long, for the equaliser came before half-time. In the second period, Leeds took the lead and it really looked like the end, yet Martin Williams made it 2-2 after 64 minutes, and with Reading continually surging forward, they scored the winner through Trevor Morley with only five minutes remaining on the clock. That victory is regarded as one of the greatest ever achieved by The Royals.

Leicester City

~ Playing Record ~

Competition	Played (Total)	Home					Away					Total	
		W	D	L	F	A	W	D	L	F	A	F	A
League	10	1	2	2	5	6	1	2	2	5	5	10	11
F.A.Cup	2	0	0	2	1	3	0	0	0	0	0	1	3
League Cup	1	0	0	0	0	0	0	0	1	0	5	0	5

With few games to choose from, probably the most striking situation involving the two clubs was the one off the pitch, rather than on it, during the 1994/95 season.

The Royals had made a good start to the 1994/95 season, and there were several clubs looking enviously at Reading, and the success of their manager Mark McGhee. But buoyed by the response of the fans who pleaded for him to stay, his devotion to the Reading cause appeared beyond doubt on Tuesday the 13th of December. Struggling Premier League side Leicester City had reputedly offered to double McGhee's salary if he were to join them, but that day he confirmed that he had turned the offer down. Yet less than 24 hours later he was packing his bags for Filbert Street, not only that but Coach Colin Lee and Youth Manager Mick Hickman were joining him. John Madjeski was livid: *"Whatever happened to honour and trust"*, he stated.

Yet perhaps justice was done in the eyes of the Reading contingent, for at the end of the season Leicester were relegated, whilst - even without their early season successful manager - The Royals just missed changing places with them when they so narrowly lost in the play-off Final at Wembley.

Leyton

The

Biscuitmen

~ *Playing Record* ~

Competition	Played (Total)	Home					Away					Total	
		W	D	L	F	A	W	D	L	F	A	F	A
F.A.Cup	1	1	0	0	6	0	0	0	0	0	0	6	0

Not to be confused with their Football League counterparts, Leyton F.C. also from the East side of London, currently operate in the Ryman League Premier Division, but at one time they were a powerful force. The club in fact claims to be the oldest in London, having first seen the light of day in 1868, three years earlier than Reading.

By the early years of the 20th century the two clubs were on a par, and for several seasons regularly played each other in the Southern League. In fact it was the Londoners who gained the upperhand in most of these matches between 1906 and 1912.

Since 1920, the two have only met once, and that was - inevitably - in the F.A.Cup. At the time, the 1925/26 season, The Biscuitmen had made a steady start and were in fact en route to the Championship of the Third Division South. However, in the F.A.Cup it had not been all plain sailing, and in fact it had taken three attempts to overcome non-League Torquay United. Leyton, then playing in the Amateur London League, came to Elm Park with high hopes, but it wasn't to be, for the home side comfortably brushed aside the opposition to the tune of 6-0.

Leyton Orient

The
Biscuitmen

~ Playing Record ~

Competition	Played (Total)	Home					Away					Total	
		W	D	L	F	A	W	D	L	F	A	F	A
League	64	19	8	5	73	29	7	10	15	44	60	117	89
F.A.Cup	2	1	0	0	3	0	0	0	1	0	1	3	1
League Cup	2	0	0	1	0	2	0	1	0	1	1	1	3

The match at home to the Londoners on the 12th of February 1949 is particularly memorable, although not for the game itself. Reading were in with a chance of the Third Division South Championship that season, but in fact finished as runners-up. Goalscoring was generally left to 'Tony' MacPhee, who became the all-time record goalscorer for the club, although the majority were scored during the War years.

However, a temporary replacement for MacPhee had to be found as he was suspended for 14 days, following a (rare at this time) dismissal. Ron Blackman, a £10 signing from Gosport Borough, had only made five League appearances (and scored just one goal) in the previous two seasons, was given his chance. Ron grabbed it by netting a hat-trick against Leyton Orient at Elm Park on February the 12th, and this match was the start of a highly successful career with Reading. He replaced the, by now, veteran MacPhee, appearing as centre-forward in the remaining 16 games that season, although only adding another six goals to his total. But he then led the goalscoring charts for the club during the next five seasons (finishing as the Division's leading marksmen in 1950/51), and eventually netted a record number of League goals (158) for the club.

Lincoln City

~ Playing Record ~

Competition	Played (Total)	Home					Away					Total	
		W	D	L	F	A	W	D	L	F	A	F	A
League	24	4	5	3	15	12	3	4	5	13	22	28	34

The Royals have met The Imps on many occasions, but the interchange of personnel is perhaps more notable than the matches themselves. Most are relatively insignificant, others not so.

Percy Freeman moved from Lincoln to Reading for £11,000 in 1973, and as at Sincil Bank he soon became a firm favourite. A notable goalscorer, he also once put the scoreboard out of action at Elm Park with an off-target shot, and on another occasion a shot brought down a washing line well outside the ground!

Keith Scott's second club was Lincoln City, before he moved to Wycombe in 1991, then Swindon. Reading was a later League club and it was a big money deal. Despite scoring in his first two games for The Royals (and also the club's first ever 'Golden Goal' in a cup-tie) he never really fulfilled the hoped for promise with the club. Despite 199 League starts, only 20 were with Reading.

There is also a notable manager tie-up, in Ian Brantfoot. After a fairly modest playing career he moved to Lincoln as Coach in 1978 and Reading five years later. His five years with the club saw him win two promotions and a major cup, thereby arguably becoming the club's most successful Manager.

Liverpool

~ Playing Record ~

Competition	Played	Home					Away					Total	
	(Total)	W	D	L	F	A	W	D	L	F	A	F	A
League	2	0	0	1	1	2	0	0	1	0	2	1	4
League Cup	1	0	0	0	0	0	0	0	1	3	4	3	4

Until the club's elevation to the Premiership the two clubs had never met in competitive football, and in view of Reading's rise to the top division - and their performances during that first season - the results of the two meetings against the Merseysiders, have to be seen as somewhat disappointing. Yet put in their true context, how many Royals' fans would have even dreamt that a few years earlier the pair would meet in competition for points?

In fact Anfield was first visited during the 2006/07 season, in October, when the two teams were drawn together in the Football League Cup. With, perhaps unfairly, little interest at this stage of the competition, both teams fielded part reserve elevens, and it looked as if Reading would pay dearly for their indifference, losing at one stage by 3-0 before a final narrow defeat of 4-3.

In the Premiership, the two matches also ended in disappointment, with a 2-0 defeat in the away fixture, followed in April with a goal conceded late in the return game at the Madejski Stadium, which produced a final 1-2 scoreline. The latter match came in a rare bad spell of the season which at this time had produced just two points in seven games.

Luton Town

Many games over the years have been played with the Bedfordshire team, starting with the club's very first season in the Southern League in 1894. However, arguably the most memorable match strictly speaking does not appear in the records of this book!

This game was in the Final of the Simod (Full Members) Cup, when an enormous following of 40,000 fans, cheering for The Royals, were present at Wembley Stadium on the 27th of March 1988. The team had fought through five rounds to reach this stage, a run that had started with a 3-1 victory at Q.P.R. before a paltry attendance of 4,004. But Luton Town of Division One were clear favourites over Reading, who were destined for relegation from the Second Division that season.

Memories of a poor season were forgotten when, before a crowd of 61,740, Reading stormed to an amazing 4-1 victory, despite first conceding a goal in the 13th minute. The Royals' goals came from Michael Gilkes, Stuart Beavon (a penalty), Mick Tait, and man of the match, Neil Smillie The Sinod Cup may not have much significance in the wide field of British football, but to the Royals fans this was without doubt their greatest, and most exciting, achievement - at least up to this date.

Ron Blackman, second left in hoops, was the surprise star of the Leyton Orient match.

Percy Freeman was a star with both Reading and Lincoln City.

(Luton Town) The four Simod Cup goalscorers (Gilkes, Tait, Beavon and Smillie).

The Trevor Senior goal against Maidstone United at Elm Park.

Cup match programme from the 1967/68 season versus Manchester City.

Despite losing, the Merthyr Press thought their team played well against Reading.

Macclesfield Town

~ Playing Record ~

Competition	Played	Home					Away					Total	
	(Total)	W	D	L	F	A	W	D	L	F	A	F	A
League	2	1	0	0	1	0	0	0	1	1	2	2	2

The Royals have only met the Cheshire team on two occasions, in League matches during the 1998/99 season, therefore this gives little scope to chose a memorable match!

The Silkmen in fact were at their peak when the two clubs met on the 26th of September, for following their promotion to the Football League two years earlier (at the expense of Hereford United), they finished second in Division Three, and therefore had just celebrated another promotion. When Reading travelled to the Moss Rose ground this wasn't their first visit to this compact ground, for they had met Chester City F.C. during the early 1990's when this club were in temporary 'exile'. In a dull September match both teams were struggling in this early season bottom of the table clash, and it was with little surprise that The Royals came away with nothing - their fifteenth successive defeat. Martin Williams scored from the penalty spot in the 2-1 loss.

By early March, Reading had climbed to mid-table, whilst Macclesfield were rooted to the bottom (and from this position were subsequently relegated). Once again it was an uninspired match, but at least a victory was the final result via a single goal from Darren Caskey.

Maidstone United

The Royals

Competition	Played (Total)	Home					Away					Total	
---	---	W	D	L	F	A	W	D	L	F	A	F	A
F.A.Cup	2	0	1	0	1	1	1	0	0	2	1	3	2

~ *Playing Record* ~

The Stones only had a brief period (three seasons) in the Football League, before folding just prior to the start of the 1992/93 season. The two clubs never met in Football League action during this period, although they had been drawn together in the first round of the League Cup that season and would have met had it not been for the Kent team's sudden demise. Therefore the only competitive meetings were in the F.A.Cup, in 1988, during Maidstone's last season before promotion to the League.

Although on paper, the non-League side were the underdogs, Reading were having a fairly poor season in the Third Division, whilst the visitors were heading for the G.M. Vauxhall Conference Championship. Therefore perhaps the 1-1 draw at Elm Park on the 10th of December in the second round was not a significant shock result. When Reading travelled to Kent the following Wednesday it must have been with some concern.

The replay was played at Watling Street, the home ground of Dartford F.C., with whom Maidstone were sharing. The attendance of 2,821 represented the biggest home crowd of the season, but there was no fairly tale ending, as The Royals safely progressed through to the third round with a 2-1 victory.

Manchester City

~ Playing Record ~

Competition	Played (Total)	Home					Away					Total	
		W	D	L	F	A	W	D	L	F	A	F	A
League	14	4	1	2	9	6	2	1	4	6	12	15	18
F.A.Cup	4	0	0	2	0	11	0	2	0	1	1	1	12
League Cup	2	0	0	1	1	2	0	1	0	1	1	2	3

Prior to the 2006/07 season, the two clubs had met, perhaps somewhat surprisingly, in 12 League encounters. But the match that sticks out most in many older supporters' eyes is the F.A.Cup clash in the 1967/68 season, although it was their opponents ability rather than their own that remains in the memory. Reading had already overcome modest opposition in the first two rounds, in Aldershot and non-League Dagenham - albeit the latter in a replay.

Drawn to play at Maine Road, gave little cause for hope for the modest Third Division side versus the soon-to-be Football League Champions, but a good financial payout was guaranteed. Against all the odds, the Reading defence subdued a prolific scoring City attack force, and even a dubious penalty for the homesters was missed near the end.

For the replay an all-ticket capacity crowd saw probably the most dynamic displays of attacking football ever seen at Elm Park - unfortunately it was the opponents who performed this feat! The final score was 7-0, and it was doubtful if any club in the country could have withstood the onslaught. But at least The Biscuitmen had held their worthy opponents in one game, and earned some much needed cash from the two games which in total attracted nearly 66,000 spectators.

Manchester United

~ Playing Record ~

Competition	Played	Home					Away					Total	
	(Total)	W	D	L	F	A	W	D	L	F	A	F	A
League	2	0	1	0	1	1	0	0	1	2	3	3	4
* F.A.Cup	10	0	2	3	5	11	$1	2	2	6	9	11	20

Manchester United versus Reading - who could ever have imagined that this would one day be on the fixture list as a League match! It happened on the 23rd September 2006, when the game was played at the Madejski Stadium before a crowd of over 24,000. Kevin Doyle's 48th minute penalty was equalised by United's Ronaldo, but a 1-1 draw was hardly a disgrace against the country's top side. The team showed that with virtually the same as that of the previous season in the Championship, they could hold their own against the best. The point ensured The Royals 7th place in the table after having played six games.

In the return at Old Trafford in late December (before an attendance of 75,910), Ibrahima Sonko's 38th minute headed goal equalised United's opener of a few minutes earlier. Unfortunately The Royals were subjected to a second half onslaught, and their cause was not helped with a second booking for Sam Sodje (who had come on as a substitute) and consequently his sending off. Down to ten men there was little chance of a shock result, but a final scoreline of 2-3, with a late second consolation goal from Leroy Lita, was again a notable achievement in the circumstances.

Mansfield Town

~ Playing Record ~

Competition	Played (Total)	Home					Away					Total	
		W	D	L	F	A	W	D	L	F	A	F	A
League	48	20	4	0	51	20	2	12	10	32	43	83	63
League Cup	2	1	0	0	4	3	0	0	1	2	4	6	7

There are a large number of games from which to chose from of those against the Nottinghamshire club, yet possibly the most notable was, ironically, in 1931/32, the season when the pair first met in a League match.

In October 1931, Mansfield were easily beaten 4-1 in the Elm Park home fixture, but the return at Field Mill on the 12th of March produced an amazing score, which completed the 'double' for Reading. Although The Biscuitmen were going hard for promotion (they in fact eventually finished second) and The Town were struggling, the latter nonetheless had a reasonably good home record. Yet who would have forecast a 7-1 victory to the visitors.

The star of the Reading team was 22 year old Jack Palethorpe. Although previously considered a reserve team player, that season he was beginning to make his mark, and in fact from his 28 League matches he finished as top goalscorer with 23. Against Mansfield he netted an amazing hat-trick with all three scored within a frantic seven minute period. This set a new record time for such a feat, until Trevor Senior scored three in just four minutes, in his home debut and opening home match against Stockport County in 1983.

Merthyr Town/Tydfil

The

Biscuitmen

~ Playing Record ~

Competition	Played	Home					Away					Total	
	(Total)	W	D	L	F	A	W	D	L	F	A	F	A
League	12	5	1	0	14	2	0	3	3	4	10	18	12
F.A.Cup	1	0	0	0	0	0	1	0	0	3	1	3	1

It may surprise some supporters that the two teams, in the early League years, played so many games (12). Later, the reformed Tydfil club, based at the same ground in Merthyr were also encountered once in the F.A.Cup.

The Cup match in question came not long after the demise (in 1934) of the original Merthyr team, and during the second season of the post-War reformed club. In September 1945, they entered the Welsh League, where they attracted amazing attendances of up to 10,000, before being accepted into the Southern League for the 1946/47 season.

Merthyr had already won six Cup matches to reach the second round proper, and on the 14th of December 1946, were urged on by a record-breaking 19,000 crowd at Penydarren Park. Despite the partisan support, The Biscuitmen proved themselves to be overall the better team, and took the lead after just five minutes. The non-Leaguers missed several opportunities to equalise and generally gave a good account of themselves, before their efforts were rewarded on the stroke of half-time with the equaliser. But Reading retained the upper hand in the second period, scoring a disputed second goal and rounding their display off from the penalty spot. Reading won through 3-1 in what could have been a very tricky tie.

Middlesbrough

The

Biscuitmen

| Competition | Played | Home | | | | | Away | | | | | Total | |
	(Total)	W	D	L	F	A	W	D	L	F	A	F	A
League	14	2	3	2	8	8	1	3	3	4	13	12	20
League Cup	1	0	0	1	0	1	0	0	0	0	0	0	1

~ Playing Record ~

Two players, nearly seventy years apart, were signed from the north-east club, and both played a significant role in the history of Reading F.C.

The loss of top goalscorer Joe Bailey at the end of the 1920/21 season led to the club bringing in Sam Jennings, on loan from Middlesbrough. The player finished up staying for three seasons, during which he topped the goalscoring list each time, before his eventual permanent move to West Ham. His loan stay was so long that his signing for the Hammers caused confusion as they thought he was a Reading registered player!

The second player will be far more memorable to supporters, that of Trevor Senior who returned 'home' in October 1989. Senior's initial move to Watford proved to be far from successful, and although his form improved at Ayresome Park he never really settled there. But his return to Elm Park was akin to the return of the prodigal son, and although his return transfer fee cost £150,000, part of this was paid for in the first home match when the attendance was nearly 50% up on the previous game. The results picked up, and by the season's end he became far and away the Club's leading goalscorer from his 37 League games.

Millwall

The Biscuitmen

~ Playing Record ~

Competition	Played	Home					Away					Total	
	(Total)	W	D	L	F	A	W	D	L	F	A	F	A
League	84	26	6	10	82	36	8	11	23	30	70	112	106
F.A.Cup	4	2	0	1	7	4	0	1	0	1	1	8	5
League Cup	2	0	1	0	1	1	0	0	1	3	4	4	5

A number of matches with Millwall have been acrimonious or controversial, but on a lighter note, one has to delve back to the 1932/33 season.

In the F.A.Cup that season, The Biscuitmen first beat Brentford, then three matches with Coventry City before they were finally overcome. Come the third round, and both teams were going strong in their respective divisions (Reading in the Third South and Millwall the Second) when they met on a murky, and appropriately named, Cold Blow Lane, on January the 14th. The match ran to form, for late in the second half The Lions led 2-0, but when a thick fog enveloped the ground, making it impossible to see either goal from the halfway line, the referee had no option but to abandon the match, in the 73rd minute. The players returned to their dressing rooms, with the Reading contingent congratulating themselves on their good fortune which would give them another, equal, chance. Then it was noticed that goalkeeper Dick Mellors was absent. A search was made and eventually he was found, stoically guarding his goal in the fogbound ground, unaware that the match had been abandoned a few minutes earlier!

Reading managed to hold Millwall to a 1-1 draw four days later, but lost the replay at Elm Park by 2-0.

Newcastle United

~ Playing Record ~

Competition	Played	Home					Away					Total	
	(Total)	W	D	L	F	A	W	D	L	F	A	F	A
League	2	1	0	0	1	0	0	0	1	2	3	3	3
* F.A.Cup	3	0	1	0	3	3	0	0	2	1	8	4	11
League Cup	2	1	0	0	3	1	0	0	1	0	4	3	5

Until the 2006/07 season, the two clubs had only met in a handful of cup matches.

At St James' Park on the 6th of December 2006, the pair first met contesting for points. With The Royals able to go to the dizzy heights of third place should they win, and The Geordie team having lost their previous four matches, this goal was not unrealistic. But aided by a controversial penalty decision, when they were one goal up, Reading had to eventually accept a 2-1 defeat.

The late season return had even more at stake, for a victory would provide another three points toward the unimaginable - before the season's start - a place in Europe! The match was slightly overshadowed by the return of Michael Owen to the Newcastle line-up after his horrific injury which had sidelined him for ten months, and it looked like a storybook return when he had the ball in the net after just seven minutes - but it was ruled offside. From then on Owen faded into the background as Reading pushed forward, and their efforts were rewarded in the 51st minute when Dave Kitson powered in only his second League goal for the club. The 1-0 victory lifted the club to sixth in the table.

Newport County

The **Biscuitmen**

~ Playing Record ~

Competition	Played (Total)	Home					Away					Total	
		W	D	L	F	A	W	D	L	F	A	F	A
League	80	27	6	7	90	36	7	14	19	42	68	132	104
F.A.Cup	9	2	3	0	16	8	1	0	3	4	7	20	15
League Cup	1	0	0	0	0	0	0	0	1	1	2	1	2

With eighty League games to choose from plus nine from the F.A.Cup (conversely only one meeting in the League Cup), there are a number that could be considered memorable, but the most worthy contender is the match played on the 20th August 1920. A one-nil away victory perhaps is not particularly noteworthy, but the fact that this was the two clubs first ever Football League fixture is.

The Welsh club's acceptance was somewhat fortunate, for formed only in 1912, their only experience had been three pre-war Southern League Division Two seasons, and one in the First Division, when they finished fifth from bottom. What transpired to be County's best crowd of the season, 14,500 (a new record number), turned up at Somerton Park. Despite spending virtually the whole game attacking, it was Reading that snatched the only goal of the game, when, in the 28th minute, Joe Bailey headed in Len Andrews' cross. This set-back made the Welshman even more determined, and there was no let up in the second half, during which they totally dominated the play. But a stoic display, especially from ex-Woolwich Arsenal goalkeeper Syd Crawford kept the home team at bay. Crawford later made a name for himself by saving penalties, totalling over fifty during his nine Reading years.

Sam Jennings, a three year loan
signing from Middlesbrough.

Joe Bailey, scorer of Reading's
first ever Football League goal,
at Newport County in 1920.

Kitson's goal against Newcastle United.

The first goal of the 1980/81 season, versus Northampton Town, was scored by Hetzke.

Programme from the last League match played at Elm Park, versus Norwich City.

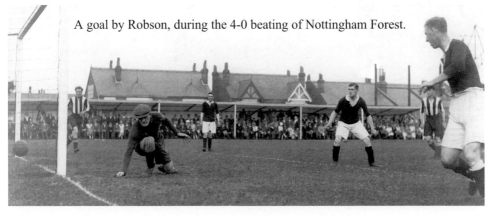

A goal by Robson, during the 4-0 beating of Nottingham Forest.

Northampton Town

~ *Playing Record* ~

Competition	Played	Home					Away					Total	
	(Total)	W	D	L	F	A	W	D	L	F	A	F	A
League	88	29	10	5	94	38	16	9	19	66	85	160	123
F.A.Cup	1	0	0	0	0	0	0	0	1	0	3	0	3
League Cup	4	1	0	1	5	3	2	0	0	4	0	9	3

With 88 League matches played with The Cobblers this represents the joint third highest number of any club. Yet despite such a wide choice of options, arguably, none of these matches produced anything exceptional, though one of the four League Cup matches provides perhaps a more appropriate choice for several reasons.

The 1980/81 season started with both the first round home and away legs of the Football League Cup, on the 8th and 13th of August. Overcoming the Fourth Division side perhaps had no particular merit, but with his early goal in the match, Steve Hetzke had the minor honour of netting the first in competitive football that season. Reading won 2-0 at the County Ground, which was enough to see them through to the next round, despite surprisingly losing the home leg 3-2. In the first leg, for such an early season match, the floodlights were probably hardly needed, which was just as well, for in Northampton's first League game the club's brand new set failed and their match versus Southend had to be abandoned!

Notable inclusions in the cup line-ups were Neil Webb, as a substitute in the second leg, and he soon became a regular member, plus youngster Kerry Dixon, a new signing from non-League Dunstable, who made his debut in the first of these matches.

Norwich City

The Biscuitmen

~ Playing Record ~

Competition	Played	Home					Away					Total	
	(Total)	W	D	L	F	A	W	D	L	F	A	F	A
League	58	15	5	9	53	39	8	8	13	39	48	92	87
* F.A.Cup	2	1	0	0	2	1	0	1	0	1	1	3	2

There are three particularly memorable matches against The Canaries. The first comes from the 1949/50 season, although the campaign was not particularly memorable in itself. But on March the 25th, aided by a Ron Blackman hat-trick - a player considered by many to be the Club's best ever centre-forward - The Biscuitmen won 4-1, yet in their remaining eight games only managed to notch up a total of seven goals. The match also saw the 'sending off' of the referee, who caused confusion with his white shirt, and was asked to cover it with a dark jacket!

Ten years later, Reading played Norwich in the F.A.Cup, a team who despite their Third Division status had reached the semi-final stage a year earlier. After a surprise draw at Carrow Road, the replay produced another exciting game. The homesters took a half-time lead through Jimmy Wheeler, then doubled the lead from a frequently remembered amazing goal. Awarded a free kick, generally regarded as at least 30 yards from the goal, 'Bomber' (nicknamed for his legendary powerful kicking) Ray Reeves scored with a low thunderous shot from an apparently insignificant position. The team went on to win the replay 2-1.

Finally, The Canaries were the last club to play a League match at Elm Park, on the 3rd of May 1998.

Nottingham Forest

The

Biscuitmen

~ Playing Record ~

Competition	Played	Home					Away					Total	
	(Total)	W	D	L	F	A	W	D	L	F	A	F	A
League	22	5	2	4	18	14	3	2	6	11	23	29	37
* F.A.Cup													

The 1925/26 season had been without doubt the club's most successful until that time, for from previous 'also-rans', the team finished at top spot in the Third Division South and hence were promoted to the Second. But the euphoria had to be controlled after the first two matches the following season were both lost.

The club's elevation naturally brought about a whole new set of clubs to be met for the first time, not least the renowned, Nottingham Forest, who had only previously been met once, in a pre-League F.A.Cup match. Despite the two earlier disappointments, well over seventeen thousand fans were at Elm Park for the match. Possibly slightly lacking in confidence, the spirits were lifted when Frank Richardson put The Biscuitmen one up early in the game, and the team went on to cap a memorable day with an unexpected 4-0 morale boosting victory. Richardson netted another in the game, and he went on to become a favourite with the fans with his 'shoot on sight' style.

However, it was a different story a few months later when Reading crashed 5-1 in the return fixture! But by the season's end the team finished in a respectable just below midway place in the table.

Notts County

The **Biscuitmen**

~ *Playing Record* ~

Competition	Played (Total)	Home					Away					Total	
		W	D	L	F	A	W	D	L	F	A	F	A
League	50	15	5	5	52	30	4	7	14	25	46	77	76
* F.A.Cup	1	0	0	0	0	0	0	0	1	2	4	2	4

Two matches versus County, one each side of the Second World War, were particularly notable.

The first, near the start of the 1936/37 season, related more to the off-field activities, for on the 5th of September (the first home Saturday match), the improved spectator facilities at the Tilehurst Road side were formally handed over. This area had been partly roofed, and in addition a clock was installed in the 'O' of the Simonds Brewery advertisement, plus cushions were made available in the grandstand. The Biscuitmen marked the occasion suitably by comfortably beating County 4-1.

Also near the start of a season, 1949/50, Reading entertained County on the 29th of September. The home team had made an indifferent start to the season, before an improvement in form, and the match in question attracted a staggering crowd officially numbering 29,092 (but more gained illegal entry). By this time Reading were heading the table, hence the enormous crowd, but this wasn't the only reason, for the visitors had in their attack up front the iconic Tommy Lawton. His signing for a Third Division club had stunned the football world and his appearances in the team increased crowd figures everywhere. The Biscuitment lost the match 1-0, and County went on to win the Third Division South Championship.

Oldham Athletic

~ *Playing Record* ~

Competition	Played	Home					Away					Total	
	(Total)	W	D	L	F	A	W	D	L	F	A	F	A
League	40	12	4	4	45	20	7	5	8	29	33	74	53
F.A.Cup	2	0	0	2	2	5	0	0	0	0	0	2	5

Several incidents centred around The 'Latics during the 1994/95 season, which in varying degrees affected the fortunes of the Berkshire club.

The campaign saw The Royals finish second in the First Division, yet denied promotion (due to reorganisation of the clubs only the top club was promoted), during which the double was achieved over their Lancashire opponents (3-1 and 2-1). But disappointment came in the shape of the F.A.Cup when they lost the third round tie 3-1 at home to the same team; ironically this was the first match of dual managers Quinn and Gooding's permanent appointments. But promotion was the main aim, and an unrequested favour was provided by Oldham.

Both Barnsley and Reading were two of the teams battling for a play-off spot (or even automatic promotion), and the Yorkshire team had a game in hand over The Royals. This match was played on the 2nd of May against Oldham, but The Tykes could only manage a 1-1 home draw, and this denied them a coveted place, but ensured Reading their play-off spot - without them even kicking a ball!

Although in the final event the shattering disappointment experienced at Wembley Stadium in the play-off final versus Bolton Wanderers will live in the memories of Reading fans forever.

Oxford United

~ *Playing Record* ~

No match nor player transfer can match the one factor that 'links' these two clubs in the most dramatic fashion; if a serious situation had been allowed to develop there would, today, be no Reading F.C. nor Oxford United F.C.

In mid-April 1983, Reading lamely fought a scoreless draw at home to Gillingham before a pathetic sub-3,000 crowd; this left The Royals perilously close to relegation from the Third Division (which they did eventually suffer). Meanwhile Oxford were doing nicely near the top of the table. Then the bombshell was announced that the Reading chairman, Frank Waller, had agreed with his Oxford counterpart, Robert Maxwell, that the two clubs would merge, and under the name of 'Thames Valley Royals', both grounds would be sold and a new one built in the Didcot area. Needless to say this outrageous plan never came to fruition with the fans of both clubs firmly against such an idea. Less than one month later the 'deal' was called off, and the Reading Chairman and his two conspirator Directors resigned.

It is ironic that 25 years later, the two clubs having continued on their own ways, Oxford United were playing back in non-League football, whilst Reading, at their peak, were four levels higher.

Peterborough United

~ Playing Record ~

Competition	Played	Home					Away					Total	
	(Total)	W	D	L	F	A	W	D	L	F	A	F	A
League	30	7	6	2	23	16	2	3	10	19	30	42	46
F.A.Cup	2	1	0	0	1	0	0	1	0	0	0	1	0
League Cup	11	2	2	1	5	3	3	2	1	7	5	12	8

Not having been elected into the Football League until 1960 has naturally limited the number of meetings between the two clubs, but the clash at the London Road ground on the 1st of February 1992 is remembered, not only for the result - despite scoring three goals, Reading lost 5-3 - but for one player making his debut for the club.

David Lee was a loan signing from Chelsea, for whom he had made occasional first team appearances from 1988. He was generally regarded as a midfield player or a centre-half, and it was in this position that he lined up at Peterborough. In that high-scoring game he scored twice, unusual in view of his playing position, but one goal was netted for each side! Even more remarkable is the fact that his loan spell at the Elm Park club was limited to just five starts (and none as substitute) - within six consecutive games - yet despite his defensive role he scored five goals in total, which by the season's end made him the joint third top League goalscorer for the club! A rate of one goal a game which any striker would be proud of.

Lee went on to play for several clubs, during which he appeared in over 170 League matches and scored 35 goals.

Plymouth Argyle

~ Playing Record ~

Competition	Played (Total)	Home					Away					Total	
		W	D	L	F	A	W	D	L	F	A	F	A
League	54	10	7	10	38	34	6	6	15	33	48	71	82
* F.A.Cup	3	1	1	0	2	1	0	0	1	0	1	2	2

One of Reading's most successful of seasons was 1925/26 when, as Champions, they were promoted to the Second Division for the first time. Two of their most important matches centred around Plymouth Argyle, their nearest challengers for the one promotion place.

The home match in October was a milestone in that this was the first match that the manager, Arthur Chadwick, actually picked the team (with the Board's approval!) Undefeated in eleven games the 1-1 draw - before a crowd of over 20,000 - was though, something of a disappointment. Reading's goalscorer that day was Hugh Davey, the leading scorer that season with 23 in just 24 matches.

The return match in late February also saw a 20,000 plus crowd, with 2,000 cheering on the visitors. Davey had just been sold to Portsmouth, but his replacement, an expensive signing from Swindon Town - Frank Richardson - was one of the goalscorers in the 3-1 victory. Two other players included in the line-up that day were Internationals Billy McConnell (Ireland) and Dai Evans (Wales) who had both been refused permission to play for their countries, the club opting for them to help their club instead. The victory at Home Park helped to seal the Championship, with Reading finishing just one point ahead of Plymouth.

Portsmouth

The

Biscuitmen

Competition	Played (Total)	Home					Away					Total	
		W	D	L	F	A	W	D	L	F	A	F	A
League	36	5	7	6	15	18	2	6	10	11	30	26	48
* F.A.Cup	3	1	0	0	3	1	1	0	1	1	3	4	4

~ Playing Record ~

Several players have made their mark, with the two clubs, amongst them:

Frank Ibbotson, a young winger from Portsmouth signed for Reading in May 1939, yet never played for the club, and quite possibly never even saw Elm Park. Within weeks he was called up to the Forces, never even having attended a training session, and tragically died from his injuries sustained in the D-Day invasion.

Ron Tindall cost a record £11,000 when he signed for Reading from West Ham in October 1952. Combining football with a career in cricket, he was never really committed to the Elm Park cause and was given a free transfer within two years in order to emigrate to South Africa. Whereupon he decided to signed for Portsmouth instead (for free!), going on to enjoy a long and successful career with them as a player and later manager.

Ray Hiron came to Elm Park from Portsmouth on a free transfer in July 1975. was made captain, and retired from the full-time game three years later. Neil Webb, arguably the best ever player born and bred in the town, moved to Pompey in July 1982 for a then record fee, whilst six years later, Trevor Senior - generally considered to be Reading's greatest ever goalscorer - made the journey in the opposite direction.

Port Vale

~ Playing Record ~

Competition	Played (Total)	Home					Away					Total	
		W	D	L	F	A	W	D	L	F	A	F	A
League	60	16	7	7	48	32	8	6	16	29	46	77	78
League Cup	2	1	0	0	1	0	0	1	0	2	2	3	2

When over 1,500 Reading fans made the relatively long journey to Port Vale in the last match of the 1978/79 season, they represented almost half the total crowd at Vale Park (3,603). For the below mid-table Potteries team it was just another meaningless end of season encounter, but for The Biscuitmen, just one point was needed for the Fourth Division Championship, promotion having already been achieved.

Despite the game being played in early May, it was accompanied by sleet and snow, but this didn't dampen the performance of the Champions-elect as they romped away with a 3-0 victory, and it could have been more had it not been for the display of the home team goalkeeper. The opener was scored by Martin Hicks, an ever-present in all the club's 57 League and cup games that season - his only goal of the season. The other goalscorers that day were the more conventional marksman Pat Earles and John Alexander, the latter who that season had found it difficult to command a regular first team place, eventually earned his place after sensationally scoring all four in the earlier home victory over Grimsby Town.

By not conceding a goal in 11 consecutive matches the club created a new Football League record.

(Above) In 1949, Reading lost at home to Notts County, with
the unmistakeable Tommy Lawton causing much of the damage!

(Below, left) Goalscorer (for each side) against Peterborough United - David Lee.
(Below right) A record fee was received when Neil Webb
(here wearing his England shirt) moved to Portsmouth.

(Right) Hick's goal in the 3-0 win over Port Vale.

(Below) The bemused Rochdale goalkeeper is told by the referee that a goal has been awarded!

GOALS!

Another Trevor Senior goal, this time versus Rotherham United.

Preston North End

Of those matches against the Lancashire team, one of particular significance follows, even if for a negative reason!

The 1982/83 season started poorly for Reading, with just one victory in the first seven games, the defeats included a 4-0 thrashing at Lincoln and an amazing 12 goal thriller (including four from Kerry Dixon) - which finished at 5-7 at Doncaster. The Elm Park faithful had already made their feelings known against Chairman Frank Waller, demanding his resignation, and they voted with their feet on October the 2nd. That day, the ground saw the depressing sight of the club's lowest ever crowd for a League match, just 1,713 faithful souls. The result didn't help, for a 3-2 defeat ensured - with both goals coming from Kerry Dixon (inevitably!). This result sent the team to the bottom of the table. But the supporters got their wish, for three days later Waller resigned. The team continued to lose more than they won, although by the last away match even a point at Deepdale, Preston, may have saved them; but The Royals lost 2-0.

Although not in the confines of this book, another adverse record worth noting (?), is the club's worst ever defeat which came in the 1893/94 season when Reading lost 18-0 at Deepdale in the first round of the F.A.Cup.

Queens Park Rangers

The Biscuitmen

~ Playing Record ~

Competition	Played (Total)	Home					Away					Total	
		W	D	L	F	A	W	D	L	F	A	F	A
League	72	24	6	6	69	35	10	9	17	41	55	110	90
* F.A.Cup													
League Cup	1	1	0	0	4	0	0	0	0	0	0	4	0

The 1960/61 season was a far from happy one, for the team generally hovered around the Third Division relegation zone throughout. April was an incredibly busy period, with nine League games, and with three left to play a victory against The Rangers at Elm Park on the 26th of April was vital.

The importance of the match nearly doubled the seasonal average gate of 7,692, and with the visitors laying in third place, they were promotion hopefuls. A perfect start was made with an early goal from top goalscorer Jimmy Wheeler, his 28th League goal of the season, then tragedy struck when the marksmen was carried off unconscious after a collision. Down to 10 men, no substitutes in those days, The Biscuitmen gamely hung on, but just before half-time they finally conceded the equaliser.

The crowd were amazed when Wheeler, re-appeared for the second half, although clearly far from fully fit. But with grit and determination he chased and fought for every ball, before being rewarded with a second goal on 64 minutes. Rangers fought strongly for the equaliser, before a third Reading goal - a fantastic 20 yard shot - from Chris Palethorpe secured the two points.

Another home win, plus a defeat, followed, that finally saw Reading avoid the drop by just two points.

Rochdale

~ Playing Record ~

Competition	Played	Home					Away					Total	
	(Total)	W	D	L	F	A	W	D	L	F	A	F	A
League	16	6	2	0	15	5	2	1	5	7	11	22	16

Most of the 1970's were spent in the old Fourth Division, generally a grim period in the club's history. Most of the matches against The 'Dale were during this time and three were particularly notable for totally different reasons.

In the 1974/75 season, with the late season match at Elm Park heading for a draw, extrovert Robin Friday scored the winner, then celebrated by running around behind the goal, and giving a poor, unsuspecting, policeman a big kiss! The opening match of the next season, produced what has become known as 'The goal that never was'. After only ten minutes, Tommy Youlden attempted a speculative shot from a 30 yard free kick which sailed narrowly past the upright. Then to everybody's amazement the referee, Mr. W.C.Harvey (his debut match in the Football League), pointed to the centre spot - awarding a goal which was of course hotly disputed by the Rochdale players, but not the nearest linesman.

Towards the end of the 1977/78 season, Rochdale, bottom of the table and heading for another re-election application, 'attracted' a crowd of just 734 for the Reading game (their lowest ever was 588 in 1974), this attendance being the lowest The Royals have ever played before in the League.

Rotherham United

The Royals

Competition	Played (Total)	Home					Away					Total	
		W	D	L	F	A	W	D	L	F	A	F	A
League	36	11	6	1	27	13	4	6	8	21	31	48	44
League Cup	3	2	0	0	5	2	0	1	0	2	2	7	4

~ Playing Record ~

Notable experiences concerning the two clubs often relate to personnel rather than matches.

In the relegation season of 1970/71, Reading brought on Ray Flannigan as a substitute in the home game, but his actual involvement in the match was delayed, for on removing his track suit his long hair got tangled up with it! Four seasons later, two Reading players - Dick Habbin and Barrie Wagstaff - wanted a move away from Elm Park, and eventually the Football League set fees on both. But with no suitable offers for either player, both went for £10,000 - at what was regarded as 'ridiculous prices' in the circumstances - a quarter the original Tribunal figure for free-scoring Habbin. Rotherham was the benefactor.

In the first match of the 1984/85 season, Trevor Senior scored (the winner) against Rotherham, on his debut, after less than two minutes from the start. The following season, in March, also at home to the Millmoor club, Terry Hurlock was sent off and Martin Hicks suffered a fractured jaw that kept him out for the remaining games that season.

Finally, Ian Porterfield, one of Reading's most successful of managers, was previously a loan player with the club, and first saw success in a managerial role with Rotherham.

Scunthorpe United

The

Biscuitmen

Competition	Played	Home					Away					Total	
	(Total)	W	D	L	F	A	W	D	L	F	A	F	A
League	22	7	3	1	16	4	5	3	3	14	10	30	14

~ *Playing Record* ~

One of the most controversial goals ever scored at Elm Park was seen during the 1964/65 season.

The early season match, played on the 12th of September, saw Reading desperately defending their slender one goal lead, when former England Youth Player, John Petts, was adjudged by the referee to have handled the ball, and he awarded a penalty to the visitors. Inevitably the Reading players surrounded the referee, and their prolonged protests eventually resulted in the official consulting with his nearest linesman. After some discussion, the original decision was reversed, which resulted in the referee deciding on a 'dropped ball' (bounce-up) instead.

Maurice Evans came away with the ball, whilst the Scunthorpe players were still remonstrating against the referee's decision reversal. A long clearance upfield caught the Scunthorpe defence off-guard, allowing Thornhill a clear path to net his second goal of the match. Reading won the match 2-0.

Although initially a defensive player, Thornhill had moved up from half-back to inside right that season. He scored in the next match, against Queens Park Rangers (a 5-3 home win) and two weeks after the Scunthorpe game he netted four goals in the 6-2 trouncing of Watford, yet only managed one more in League matches that season.

Sheffield United

~ Playing Record ~

Competition	Played (Total)	Home					Away					Total	
		W	D	L	F	A	W	D	L	F	A	F	A
League	30	10	1	4	19	19	4	5	6	15	24	34	38
F.A.Cup	1	0	0	0	0	0	0	0	1	0	1	0	1
League Cup	1	1	0	0	2	0	0	0	0	0	0	2	0

Reading played three games against the 'Blades during the Championship winning Championship season of 2005/06, and although the Yorkshire team were to finish in the runners-up spot - albeit a clear 16 points behind - The Royals had the upper hand.

The first meeting came on the 1st of October, when Reading produced some wonderful football early on and went ahead through Brynjar Gunnarsson. The visitors equalised on 15 minutes, and the match moved on to controversial refereeing decisions, a not unusual outburst from United manager Warnock, and the winning goal, another from Gunnarrson, one minute before the end. The Blades were still top of the table after the match, but Reading were closing in, now having gone eleven League games without defeat.

Less than four weeks later the Sheffield team returned for a League Cup match. The visitors still led The Royals by one point in the Championship, and this match had something of a second feature about it, with both teams making changes from their normal line-ups. But another 2-0 victory - now 17 games without defeat in all matches - saw Reading through.

The return League match in March produced a draw, and kept Reading 12 points ahead of their second placed rivals. But if Dave Kitson had converted a last minute penalty it could have been 14!

Sheffield Wednesday

The

Biscuitmen

Competition	Played (Total)	Home					Away					Total	
		W	D	L	F	A	W	D	L	F	A	F	A
League	8	2	0	2	4	4	0	2	2	5	7	9	11
F.A.Cup	2	1	0	1	3	3	0	0	0	0	0	3	3

~ Playing Record ~

Arguably Reading's most notable giant-killing exploit was against the Wednesday in the 1928/29 F.A Cup competition.

Somewhat struggling in the League, The Biscuitmen had already beaten fellow Second Division team 'Spurs 2-0, in the third round before a crowd of over 26,000. The fourth round draw decreed that First Division Champions-elect Wednesday would also visit Elm Park, and on the 26th of January a massive 29,248 crowd packed into the ground. Against all the odds, and all that the visitors could throw at them, Reading held out somehow, and then to cap it all they went ahead through leading scorer Bill Johnstone, who had also netted a brace in the previous round. The goal turned out to be the winner, and a report at the time stated that this was... *"the greatest playing success in the history of Reading F.C."* , and many would argue that this sentiment is still true. Another wrote of Reading that, *"every player was a man to be proud of."*

Johnstone could be reliably expected to score F.A.Cup goals, for two years earlier he netted nine in the Semi-Final run, but even he couldn't avoid defeat in the 1929 fifth round match. At home again, this time to Aston Villa, The Biscuitment lost 3-1, the lone Reading goalscorer being Bert Oswald.

Shrewsbury Town

The

Biscuitmen

Competition	Played	Home					Away					Total	
	(Total)	W	D	L	F	A	W	D	L	F	A	F	A
League	52	14	6	6	58	34	5	7	14	30	53	88	87
F.A.Cup	2	1	0	0	1	0	0	1	0	2	2	3	2

~ Playing Record ~

The 1-0 replay home win in the 1970/71 F.A.Cup match versus The Shrews hardly conveys the drama that ensued, especially in the closing minutes of the game.

The Biscuitmen had already thrashed non-League Bishop Stortford 6-1, and in the second round just survived with a 2-2 draw at Gay Meadow, which by all accounts they should have lost. The replay was heading towards a boring scoreless draw, then the game suddenly came to life with just three minutes still on the clock. All round action that perhaps compensated for the previous dire football.

The stalemate was finally broken with a goal from Dick Habbin (that season's leading marksman), and it looked as if the match was all but over. But the visitors fought back and during the remaining few minutes, they managed to hit the bar with a goal-bound shot, then missed an easy opportunity to equalise. The latter led to a rift between two of the Shrewsbury players, and punches were thrown between the pair! Finally it appeared that the equaliser had been scored, only for it to be disallowed, which led to some heated exchanges, and the sending off of one of the visitors.

Having just scraped through, Reading went on to lose 5-0 at Watford in the third round.

Another controversial goal, scored by Thornhill versus Scunthorpe United.

A penalty was missed by Kitson against Sheffield United.

The local press celebrate Reading's shock victory.

(Top)
Habbin, who scored against Shrewsbury Town.

(Middle)
The dilapidated Wexham Park Stadium in 2007,
where The Royals drew with Slough Town in the
F.A.Cup.

(Bottom)
The eighth goal in the demolition of Southport,
scored by Chappell.

Slough Town

~ Playing Record ~													
Competition	Played	Home					Away					Total	
	(Total)	W	D	L	F	A	W	D	L	F	A	F	A
F.A.Cup	3	2	0	0	5	1	0	1	0	3	3	8	4

The F.A.Cup on occasions provides the club and its supporters the opportunity to compete with a non-League team and always a potential 'banana-skin'. In fact a forerunner of the club had first played a forerunner of the Slough club way back in 1876.

In modern times, the pair have met in two F.A. Cup years. The first, the 1973/74 competition, ran true to form with a 3-0 Elm Park victory in the first round, although Reading at the time were a humble Fourth Division club. The goals came from Les Chappell, plus Brian Bromley and Steve Hetzke, the only strikes of the season from the pair.

In the 1991/92 season The Royals were somewhat struggling in the Third Division, and a visit to Wexham Park for the first round tie in mid-November could easily have ended in embarrassment, against a team now playing in the G.M. Vauxhall Conference. 3,990 packed into the compact enclosure, and as expected it was a close fought tie which resulted in a 3-3 draw. The replay at Elm Park was also a tight affair, and Reading only won through by 2-1.

Since the early 1990's, Slough Town have suffered misfortunes, having been thrown out of the Conference, been relegated from the Ryman (Isthmian) Premier Division and even lost the use of their ground.

Southampton

The
Biscuitmen

~ Playing Record ~

Competition	Played (Total)	Home					Away					Total	
		W	D	L	F	A	W	D	L	F	A	F	A
League	30	6	4	5	19	16	2	7	6	19	28	38	44
* F.A.Cup	2	1	0	1	3	2	0	0	0	0	0	3	2
League Cup	3	1	1	0	2	1	0	0	1	0	2	2	3

It had been a modest season for The Biscuitmen, with a final 11th place to look forward to, but the visit of Southampton on Easter Monday 1960 lifted what could have been an apathetic crowd. The visitors were top of the table and were to become the eventual Champions, although their 'away' record was not the best, as Reading proved.

A huge holiday crowd of 23,692, boosted no doubt by many supporters from the Hampshire town, one of whom during the match threw a missile at goalkeeper David Jones. A possible 'situation' was quickly diffused, when David Jones calmly took a bite from it, and then threw it back into the crowd!

Jimmy Whitehouse, the 'architect' of many Reading goals via Jimmy Wheeler, put the home team into the lead to the consternation of Southampton, who really needed at least a point from the match, with Norwich City close on their heels. Then the other Jimmy (Wheeler) scored, with one of the softest of his career. A lost cause chaser, the diminutive inside-forward entered the penalty area, and tangled with Southampton's goalkeeper plus two defenders. More in hope than with conviction he made contact with the ball, and as other defenders scrambled to clear, it very slowly trickled over the goal line.

Southend United

The

Biscuitmen

~ Playing Record ~

Competition	Played (Total)	Home					Away					Total	
		W	D	L	F	A	W	D	L	F	A	F	A
League	88	27	9	8	102	54	7	12	25	46	86	148	140
F.A.Cup	3	2	0	0	5	3	0	0	1	0	2	5	5
League Cup	1	1	0	0	5	1	0	0	0	0	0	5	1

With several other clubs, the Essex club is the joint third most frequent opponent of Reading.

But amongst the many games played between the pair, those over Easter 1961 were two of the most important. Reading were struggling within the relegation zone, and were desperate for points when United were the visitors to Elm Park. The comfortable 3-0 victory that ensued was just what was needed over a fellow relegation haunted team. In contrast to a year earlier (versus Southampton) the crowd of 4,945 represented about one fifth of the gate from that previous match.

The very next day, Easter Saturday, the team travelled to Roots Hall boosted by their victory, and to everybody's surprise, not least their supporters, they completed the double, beating the seaside club by a single goal from Ray 'Bomber' Reeves from the penalty spot (repeating the same feat of 24 hours earlier). This victory not only lifted Reading out of the relegation zone, but this was their only League win away from home that season. The team won only three of their remaining seven fixtures (notably 4-0 and 5-1 at home to Brentford and Torquay respectively), to finished 18th in the table, and two points clear of the 'drop'.

Southport

The Biscuitmen

Competition	Played	Home					Away					Total	
	(Total)	W	D	L	F	A	W	D	L	F	A	F	A
League	16	5	3	0	20	5	1	2	5	10	22	30	27
* F.A.Cup	3	0	1	0	1	1	1	1	0	3	1	4	2

~ Playing Record ~

There have been comparatively few matches played against this club, now long since voted out of the Football League (in 1968). Yet several have produced some not to be forgotten clashes.

One such match was in the F.A. Cup, second round in the 1951/52 season in what became three matches - first at Haig Avenue produced a 1-1 draw as did the Elm Park replay, and the stalemate was only finally broken when Reading triumphed 2-0 at Villa Park in the second replay.   The third round produced a 3-0 home defeat to Swansea Town.

The 1969/70 season was a fairly unremarkable one, with a final finish of 8th in the Third Division. But a new competition for the start of the following season, the Watney Cup, promised to provide some money-spinning gates. Qualifying was all about scoring goals, and this is what Reading did against an already relegated Southport side, and they did it in some style, although only two were required. The last home match was won by 8-0, and included amongst the goalscorers was Gordon Cumming with a hat-trick, the first season in which four different players netted three each in a match. The score was a record joint winning margin (the other was the 10-2 over Crystal Palace in 1946).

South Shields

The
Biscuitmen

Competition	Played	Home					Away					Total	
	(Total)	W	D	L	F	A	W	D	L	F	A	F	A
League	4	2	0	0	7	2	0	1	1	0	3	7	5

~ *Playing Record* ~

With just four League games played, in the 1920's, there is not much scope to pick a special match. The pair first met in 1926, then the following season Shields were relegated to the Third Division North - although in reality they underwent a metamorphosis and became Gateshead F.C.

In the 1926/27 season, both clubs were slightly struggling, and the results in the League matches went to form, with each club wining its respective home game. Early in the following season, the situation for both clubs was even worse, for by mid-November, The Biscuitmen had won only one of their 14 League games and were rooted to the bottom of the table. South Shields were little better, having won just two games and lay one place above Reading. Therefore the fixture at Elm Park held out little hope for an exciting match. The crowd thought so too, for it numbered only 6,141, which transpired to be the lowest of the season.

But they were wrong, for Reading won 5-1, and this proved to be the best win of the season. The goalscorers were Hugh Davey with a hat-trick, his penultimate game for the club before he was sold to Portsmouth, and left-winger 'Jack' Robson who netted a brace, and also left soon after, to Derby County.

Stockport County

The 1993/94 season was one to savour, for Reading were promoted to the First Division (second level) at the end of that campaign. One of their main rivals was the Edgeley Park club, who finally finished in 4th spot, and they were the visitors to Elm Park on the 28th December. Reading were in pole position at the time, having displaced County just a couple of weeks earlier.

This top of the table clash captured the locals' imagination and they flocked to the ground to produce a gate numbering 11,420, nearly double the number at the last match at home to Huddersfield Town. At this time this was a capacity crowd, the best League attendance for six years, and over 1,000 were locked out.

Reading had become known for their tight defence around this period, having not conceded a League goal for four games, and only three in the previous eight. They extended this record with a 2-0 win, and in the process advanced their unbeaten run in the Second Division to 16 games (the previous defeat came at Wrexham in early September). Stuart Lovell scored both goals, a player always seen as a 'local' yet had in fact been born in Sidney, Australia.

Stoke City

The

Biscuitmen

~ Playing Record ~

Competition	Played (Total)	Home					Away					Total	
		W	D	L	F	A	W	D	L	F	A	F	A
League	42	10	7	4	34	20	6	4	11	19	36	53	56
* F.A.Cup	1	0	0	1	0	1	0	1	0	0	0	0	1

Going well back in time, Stoke City and Arthur Bacon are synonymous. The 1930/31 season was a hard slog throughout which ended in relegation from the Second Division for Reading. There was little of merit that could come out of such a poor season, and early season defeats by 7-1 and 8-1 did not look good for the future. By late March the situation still looked grim, until an unexpected 6-1 victory over fellow strugglers Barnsley slightly lifted the gloom.

Then, on April 3rd, Reading entertained the Potteries team. Arthur Bacon was a typical centre-forward of the period, burly and strong, who was there for one purpose - to score goals. That day he accomplished this task with aplomb, scoring no fewer than six goals of Reading's seven. Typically one goal came from a charge on the goalkeeper that finished with both in the net, and rather than a goal would have earned a booking in modern times! His sixth was the best, a terrific drive from a narrow angle that literally tore into the net, detaching it from the cross-bar. Six goals in a League game remains an individual Reading record to date.

Despite this 7-3 victory over Stoke City, Reading picked up just one more point in their final six games, and along with Cardiff City were relegated.

Sunderland

Competition	Played	Home					Away					Total	
	(Total)	W	D	L	F	A	W	D	L	F	A	F	A
League	12	3	1	2	7	5	2	2	2	7	10	14	15
F.A.Cup	3	1	0	1	3	4	0	1	0	1	1	4	5

~ Playing Record ~

Meetings with Sunderland have been few and far between, but those in the 2004/05 season, whilst not remarkable, are none the less memorable.

Reading lost out in the play-off finals in 2002, then two somewhat disappointing seasons finishes (9th and 7th respectively) in the First Division/Championship followed. The 2003/04 season saw Sunderland top the table with 94 points, when they lost few games, but two were against The Royals. On the 31st of August, at The Medejski Stadium, a Nicky Forster strike after just two minutes was enough to secure the three points, in an entertaining game that lifted the team to fifth in the League, and gave hope for the rest of the season.

By early April, there were still hopes of a play-off place for The Royals, whilst Sunderland were topping the table and well on their way to securing the Championship. But in front of the Sky TV cameras, the visitors pulled off an unexpected win. All the goals came in the second half, with the homesters taking the lead after 52 minutes, before Dave Kitson equalised with fifteen minutes remaining. With Reading now in the ascendency, a penalty eight minutes from time (Kitson again) sealed this unlikely win.

Sutton Town

The

Biscuitmen

~ Playing Record ~

Competition	Played (Total)	Home					Away					Total	
		W	D	L	F	A	W	D	L	F	A	F	A
F.A.Cup	1	0	0	0	0	0	1	0	0	2	1	2	1

The 1933/34 season was one of the earlier years in which Reading competed with a non-League club for an F.A.Cup match, Sutton Town from Nottinghamshire. To get thus far, The Biscuitmen had beaten Watford (3-0), whilst the non-Leaguers had played six teams to have reached the second round. Included in their run, the little Nottingham Combination club caused a major shock when they beat Rochdale 2-1.

The draw decreed that the game be played at The Avenue ground of Sutton, a somewhat basic venue and harshly condemned by the reporter for the Berkshire Chronicle. Reading suggested 'switching' the tie, to increase the gate, but their opponents would not budge.

A near capacity crowd of 5,166, packed the little enclosure, and in view of the dreadful weather and the partisan crowd, the task was never going to be easy. But Reading took a first half lead through Frank Newton, a prolific goalscorer (31 in only 34 appearances) whose career was tragically cut short due to injury. This spurred Sutton on, and it was only the heroics displayed by 'keeper Percy Whittaker, that prevented their opponents scoring more than one goal. But Reading scraped through what transpired to be a very sporting game, courtesy of a second goal from inside-forward 'Jack' Oxberry.

Swansea City

The
Biscuitmen

~ Playing Record ~

Competition	Played	Home					Away					Total	
	(Total)	W	D	L	F	A	W	D	L	F	A	F	A
League	56	17	4	7	51	29	9	4	15	38	56	89	85
F.A.Cup	5	0	1	1	1	4	2	0	1	5	5	6	9
League Cup	3	2	0	0	5	1	0	1	0	1	1	6	2

The 1948/49 season saw the Welsh team promoted as Champions, whilst Reading lost out by finishing as runners-up. Midway through the season the pair played each other over the Christmas matches, a fixtures tradition at this time. Mid-table Reading entertained the leaders on Christmas Day, and although not showing an over abundance of holiday good spirit, and despite a 2-0 home defeat, there was nothing to suggest there would be disciplinary problems for the return match two days later.

Played before a then record attendance of 27,508, it turned out to be one full of fouls, kicking (of each other) and pushing. One incident in the first half saw a mass 21 man brawl (the Swansea 'keeper remaining aloof), following a penalty save by George Marks, from Welsh International Roy Paul. But far worse was to come when both teams had two players sent off - a game in the 1940's (not the 1990's) - and with Reading's Ron Moyse being carried off injured The Biscuitmen finished the match with eight players. In the previous 21 years, Reading had had only three players dismissed in total!

This infamous match though actually finished in a 2-1 Reading defeat, the goalscorer being George Cryle, one of only two goals for the club in his eight game career.

(Above) Arthur Bacon, a
prolific goalscorer against
Stoke City.

(Right)
Goalkeeper Percy Whittaker,
the hero against Sutton Town.

Swindon Town's 'keeper, Allan
scores an 'own goal' for Reading.

Reading visited Thames Association's massive ground (above) just once.

(Right) Sidwell celebrates after scoring against Tottenham.

(Below) Robin Friday who, against Tranmere Rovers, scored arguably the best ever Elm Park goal.

Swindon Town

Competition	Played	Home					Away					Total	
	(Total)	W	D	L	F	A	W	D	L	F	A	F	A
League	92	27	9	10	91	51	8	16	22	40	76	131	127
* F.A.Cup	3	1	0	0	1	0	0	0	2	2	8	3	8

~ Playing Record ~

It is fitting that The Royals' fiercest local rivals over the decades has also produced so many League encounters, but it is young players, in the 1980's, that are highlighted here.

After a reasonable start to the 1980/81 season, the fourth match brought Swindon to Elm Park, and a 4-1 victory was the result. In the team that day, a young Kerry Dixon scored his second goal for the club, his debut strike coming in the previous game. Neil Webb, son of former Reading player Douggie Webb, who became arguably the best ever local born and bred player with the club, made his debut in the Swindon game. At just over 17 years and one month, he was named in the squad for the previous match, making him the youngest ever (unused) substitute for the club, and when he scored against Swindon, he became the youngest ever goalscorer for them.

In the same fixture the following season, both of Reading's goalkeepers were unavailable, and Andover's 17 year old Colin Court was signed on in the emergency. Despite having a good game, a mistake resulted in him being credited with Swindon's goal, then his opposite number, Jimmy Allen, made a similar error. Surely the only match in which 'own goals' have been 'awarded' to the two goalkeepers!

Thames Association

Competition	Played (Total)	Home					Away					Total	
		W	D	L	F	A	W	D	L	F	A	F	A
League	2	1	0	0	5	1	0	1	0	0	0	5	1

~ *Playing Record* ~

The

Biscuitmen

Who, the reader may well ask! In fact this club from East London played in the Third Division South for two seasons. Reading were relegated from the Second in 1931, and that season Thames took over Aldershot's place in the League. This was a controversial election, since Thames had no track record to speak of (just two moderate Southern League seasons) and were based in the already competitive for support 'Spurs/Arsenal/West Ham stronghold of the capital. Thames had a miserable debut season in the League finishing 20th of 22 clubs, and a year later were voted out after finishing rock bottom. Their massive West Ham Stadium at Custom House, with a claimed capacity for 120,000, rarely saw more than 3,000 at the football club's matches.

On the 10th of October 1931, Reading fought out an uninspiring scoreless draw at Custom House before an unusually large crowd numbering 4,919. In the return match, in January, The Biscuitmen comfortably disposed of their visitors with a score of 5-1. Scotsman Alex Ritchie netted a hat-trick in the match, when one shot was so powerful that it hit both posts and the crossbar before flying into the net. Ex-Arsenal player Charlie Barley, and an 'own goal' completed the scoring for Reading.

Torquay United

The

Royals

~ Playing Record ~

Competition	Played	Home					Away					Total	
	(Total)	W	D	L	F	A	W	D	L	F	A	F	A
League	70	24	8	3	93	38	6	15	14	47	58	140	96
F.A.Cup	5	0	2	0	1	1	2	1	0	5	2	6	3
League Cup	2	1	0	0	3	1	1	0	0	1	0	4	1

The early 1990's were not a very fertile period for Reading. Mid-table finishes were the order at the end of the day, and the 1991/92 season left little to enthuse over.

March and early April were particularly barren, with just two wins in nine matches, and in the last five not a single goal was scored. Many fans decided to give the Torquay home match, on April the 11th, a miss and only 3,111 bothered to turn up to see what turned out to be a goal feast. The visitors were a struggling team, with not a single victory on their travels and they were eventually relegated.

The Royals stormed to a 6-1 win, with five different goalscorers, four of whom were not renowned in this department. Lea Barkus, with only a handful of appearances for the club, scored his only League goal, Kevin Dillon in 29 League outings netted just his third of the season, and Australian born Stuart Lovell his fourth. Player/Manager Mark McGhee scored only his second of the season, but in the remaining few games managed another three, and finally the only traditional goalscorer of the quintet, Craig Maskell added two to his total, and with a modest 16 led the field in goals at the end of the campaign.

Tottenham Hotspur

~ Playing Record ~

Competition	Played	Home					Away					Total	
	(Total)	W	D	L	F	A	W	D	L	F	A	F	A
League	8	3	0	1	11	6	0	2	2	3	10	14	16
* F.A.Cup	1	1	0	0	2	0	0	0	0	0	0	2	0

Matches with the 'Spurs in the Football League and the Cups have been few and far between, despite encounters in the early days when both were members of the Southern League.

Like every match of the 2006/07 season, the home encounter with the East London team was something to look forward to. The Royals having started the season brightly had fallen back somewhat, and by the 12th of November, they lay in 11th place in the Premiership (their second lowest of the campaign), with 'Spurs just below them. Four successive defeats had led to this relatively poor position. When Keane gave the visitors the lead after 24 minutes the prospects didn't look good. But, in spite of some strange refereeing decisions, not in their favour, Reading equalised though Nicky Shorey in the 38th minute.

The match now swung in favour of the Royals, and they were rewarded with a goal from the hard-working Steve Sidwell on the stroke of half-time. The Royals continued to dominate the match, with The 'Spurs becoming ever more desperate, and just when it looked as if they might get the equaliser, Kevin Doyle put it beyond their reach with a third strike, 11 minutes before the end.

This victory lifted Reading three places up the table.

Tranmere Rovers

~ Playing Record ~

Competition	Played	Home					Away					Total	
	(Total)	W	D	L	F	A	W	D	L	F	A	F	A
# League	34	10	4	3	30	15	4	5	8	21	29	51	44
F.A.Cup	2	1	0	0	2	1	0	1	0	1	1	3	2

Any Royals supporter from at least the mid-1970's would have no doubt in nominating the most memorable match against the South Merseyside club.

The 1975/76 season was spent in the Fourth Division. On the last day of March, and hovering around the promotion positions, they entertained Tranmere. As expected it was a close fought battle, and after 69 minutes, although Reading were two goals up, there was no reason to relax. Then the enigmatic Robin Friday came into the picture and scored what was arguably the best ever goal seen at Elm Park. Received a long clearance and at head height, he controlled the ball with his foot, brought it down, and despite being surrounded by three players, swivelled, and volleyed it into the net. *"So stunning in its execution that it will surely be talked about as long as football is played at Elm Park,"* the local pressman enthused.

This spurred Reading on, and two more goals in the last 30 minutes ensured a morale boosting 5-0 victory. Friday scored a brace of goals that evening, and John Murray - including two penalties - netted his second hat-trick of the season.

The team managed just three more wins in their final seven games, and only a 3-1 last match victory over Crewe ensured their promotion.

Walsall

The Biscuitmen

~ Playing Record ~

Competition	Played (Total)	Home					Away					Total	
		W	D	L	F	A	W	D	L	F	A	F	A
# League	70	13	12	10	47	37	8	10	17	41	71	88	108
F.A.Cup	3	1	<1	0	2	1	0	1	0	0	0	2	1

Matches against Walsall are not normally relished by Reading fans, for in the 70 League matches between the two, the majority of the points have gone The Saddlers way.

The Fellows Park match in the 1964/65 season was typical of this record. An early season visit to the Midlands was expected to be an easy two points for the visitors, as they were hovering around the promotion spots following five victories in their opening eight games. Walsall were bottom of the table at the time and a poor crowd of only 3,600 was present. One factor that wasn't recognised was that of Walsall's young marksman Allan Clarke. In a struggling team he netted a hat-trick that day, and a goal from the much travelled Pat Terry, was all The Biscuitmen could offer in a final 4-1 defeat. The misery went further, for Gordon Neate suffered a bad injury which was to end his playing career.

That season was one of frustration, with the team finishing in a mid-Third Division table position, and injuries to key players that halted any real progress. Jimmy Wheeler broke his leg in September, and two other influential players - Mick Travers and Maurice Evans - also missed large parts of the season.

Watford

~ Playing Record ~

Competition	Played (Total)	Home					Away					Total	
		W	D	L	F	A	W	D	L	F	A	F	A
League	88	29	9	6	96	37	7	8	29	37	82	133	119
F.A.Cup	5	1	0	1	3	3	1	1	1	4	6	7	9
League Cup	11	2	1	2	4	7	1	2	3	8	15	12	22

Reading made a poor overall start to the 1962/63 season (apart from winning their opening game 5-0), and the 4-0 defeat at Watford didn't help. Another notable misfortune against the Hertfordshire club came the next season, with the broken leg sustained by injury-prone Jimmy Martin, which ended his full-time football career. This was the result of an innocent clash with Watford's young goalkeeper, Pat Jennings. Four years later, Reading's manager Roy Bentley signed winger George Harris from the Hertfordshire club for a bargain £1,500. Harris had the remarkable ability of scoring many goals - with his head. He became the club's leading goalscorer that season with 24 in the League.

A shock move early in the 1987/88 season saw Royals fans favourite Trevor Senior move to Vicarage Road for £325,000, but despite being arguably Elm Park's greatest goalscorer he never displayed this ability to the full after moving. A big move in the opposite direction during 1994/95 saw Lee Nogan move to Elm Park for a then joint record transfer fee of £250,000.

Finally, Peter Castle made his debut at Watford in the penultimate game of the 2002/03 season (a 3-0 victory), but only after getting his school's headmaster's permission - at 16 years and 49 days old, he became the youngest ever Football League player for Reading.

Wealdstone

The Royals

Competition	Played (Total)	Home					Away					Total	
		W	D	L	F	A	W	D	L	F	A	F	A
F.A.Cup	3	2	0	0	2	0	0	0	1	1	2	3	2

~ Playing Record ~

Controversy has surrounded all three meetings in the F.A.Cup between the pair.

A home first round draw in the 1976/77 season provided some relief from a season which ended in relegation, the Southern League side having enjoyed four victories to have reached that stage. The visitors played well, but John Murray scored from an easy chance at close range. Reading became more dominant, before Wealdstone were reduced to nine men with two second yellow cards. Yet a strong fightback nearly produced an equaliser in the closing minutes.

One year later the two clubs met again, this time at Lower Mead, and before a crowd numbering 4,044 the non-League team got their revenge. The homesters took the lead after just five minutes, and well into the second half scored again from a twice taken penalty. Reading soon pulled one back, but were unable to equalise in the last twenty frantic minutes, and so Wealdstone made the headlines in the newspapers the next day.

The third meeting in 1985/86 was another stormy affair. Reading won 1-0 at Elm Park, three players were sent off - two from Wealdstone - after a 20 man brawl, which followed a terrible tackle on Martin Hicks. The player? One Vinnie Jones, who had just come on as a substitute!

Welling United

The Royals

~ *Playing Record* ~

Competition	Played	Home					Away					Total	
	(Total)	W	D	L	F	A	W	D	L	F	A	F	A
F.A.Cup	5	1	2	0	1	0	1	1	0	3	2	4	2

The pair have only met twice, in the F.A.Cup, but the first encounter was a very long and drawn out tie, stretching to four games. In all, The Royals played ten F.A.Cup games that season yet only reached the fourth round!

After a scoreless draw on the 9th of December 1989 at Elm Park, the replay looked to be a grim prospect for The Royals. At the Conference club's home in Kent, Stuart Beavon scored from the penalty spot early in the second half, but this was equalised two minutes later. The second replay, at Elm Park six days later, produced a paltry crowd of little more than 4,000, and the result was another scoreless draw, again after extra time.

The tie was finally settled at Welling's compact Park View Road, but even then it was a narrow affair. The home team took the lead after 29 minutes, much to the delight of most of the 2,737 crowd. But at last Reading's pedigree came through and two second half goals from Steve Moran eventually sealed the tie. The facts: 420 minutes, just five goals, with none scored at Elm Park (in half of that time)!

In the 2001/02 season, a routine 1-0 victory at Elm Park ensued, when a Jamie Cureton goal was all that separated the two.

West Bromwich Albion

Despite their poor League form during the 1995/96 First Division season, The Royals had a good run in the Football League Cup which only finished in a 2-1 defeat at Leeds in the 5th round.

In the first of the two legged first round matches, against West Brom., a goal by Stuart Lovell produced a home draw, which left a big task to undertake at The Hawthorns for the second leg. But an exceptional performance, plus goals from Stuart Lovell (again), a brace from player/manager Jimmy Quinn and James Lambert, produced a well deserved but unexpected 4-2 victory (5-3 on aggregate).

The tall Quinn had made his name with Reading with his record-breaking 35 League goals two seasons earlier. After taking over the dual manager's job (with Mick Gooding), he continued as a player. Later in his career he also earned the nickname of 'Super-sub' (making over 100 League appearances from the bench), twice as an emergency goalkeeper. The first occasion came just a few weeks after the West Brom victory, when against the same team he was called into action after an injury to goalkeeper Simon Sheppard. Quinn didn't let the side down and kept a clean sheet, in a game The Royals won by 3-1.

(Above) Martin Hicks, who was injured in an unsavoury F.A.Cup match with non-League Wealdstone.

(Right) Steve Moran, who scored two goals in the 4th game versus Welling United.

Jimmy Quinn, in his early days as a Manager, scored two goals against West Bromwich Albion.

(Above left) Stuart Lovell was in the Reading youth team
that beat their Weymouth counterparts 15-0.
(Above right) Later a successful manager, Sanchez
played for both Reading and Wimbledon.
(Below) Cureton waits to pounce in the Wolves match.

West Ham United

~ Playing Record ~

Competition	Played	Home				Away					Total	
	(Total)	W	D	L	F	A	W	D	L	F	A	F	A
League	6	3	0	0	11	1	1	0	2	1	2	12	3
League Cup	1	0	>1	0	0	0	0	0	0	0	0	0	0

With just a handful of League matches there are few matches to reflect on between the two clubs. But the one other match, in the 2001/02 season League Cup competition, had plenty of drama.

The Royals had easily disposed of Luton (4-0) in the first round, and the next tie was against the Premiership team. Although often maligned, this match attracted over 21,000 to the Madejski Stadium, although on a sombre note it was played on the 11th September 2001, a date that will be remembered, worldwide, forever.

Whilst the game might have lacked goals (at least for the first 120 minutes!), it didn't lack drama, and the team's eventual victory, as the players confidence grew over their more illustrious opponents, was well deserved. The stalemate was nearly broken late in the second period of extra time, but Reading failed, and the game was destined to go to a penalty shoot-out. Reading's first shot just sneaked in off the post, then at 4-3 to the visitors, their fifth attempt was expected to finish the match. But it was missed. Now into 'sudden death', and the score rose to 5-5. Minto's effort was saved by Phil Whithead, and late substitute Adrian Viveash made it a night to remember when he fired his shot home. Reading had won 6-5 on penalties.

Weymouth

The

Biscuitmen

~ Playing Record ~

Competition	Played (Total)	Home					Away					Total	
		W	D	L	F	A	W	D	L	F	A	F	A
F.A.Cup	2	1	1	0	9	4	0	0	0	0	0	9	4

The clubs may have only met in the F.A.Cup once, way back in the 1926/27 season, but this was a memorable encounter. The Dorset team at the time were struggling in the Western League Division One (they finished bottom that season) and when The Biscuitmen drew them at home, a victory looked to be a formality. Reading took the lead after five minutes, but were then rocked, for 15 minutes later the scoreline showed the non-Leaguers 3-1 ahead. The homesters then netted two more before half-time, to complete an exciting first period with six goals on the scoresheet. But Weymouth weren't finished, for they took the lead again in the second half, before an equaliser finished the scoring at 4-4.

Weymouth decided to forego home advantage for the replay, and held their League opponents at bay until half-time. But fitness counted in the end, and Reading romped away to an eventual 5-0 - somewhat flattering - victory.

At a different level, in the 1987/88 season, the two teams were drawn together in the F.A.Youth Cup. This time there was no compromise, for The Royals thrashed The Terras by a record 15-0. Reading players in that match included Stuart Lovell, Scott Taylor and Adrian Williams, who later between them made 650 appearances for the club in the Football League.

Wigan Athletic

~ Playing Record ~

Competition	Played (Total)	Home					Away					Total	
		W	D	L	F	A	W	D	L	F	A	F	A
# League	32	10	2	4	24	15	2	5	9	13	26	37	41

The pair first met in a Division Four match in 1978, and in the 2001/02 season both competed in Division Two (the third level). Reading were promoted that year and Wigan finished around mid-table. Yet who, from either set of supporters, could have dreamt that just four years later they would be meeting in The Premiership!

The matches that season resulted in honours even, with The Royals losing 1-0 in Lancashire, and winning 3-2 at home. Despite the scoreline, Reading were easily beaten in this early season encounter, and after just three matches lay 13th in the table. But the situation was a lot brighter four months later, when the two met in the return match on the 30th of January 2007. However, The Royals fell behind to an early Heskey strike (the goalscorer in the previous encounter), but had levelled the score by half-time. After missing a good chance in the second half, Shane Long made amends with a headed goal after 53 minutes, and when Leroy Lita added a third just two minutes before the end, it looked like a reasonably comfortable victory. But Landzaat's last minute goal gave a more balanced final score, in a match that secured three points but was certainly not one of Reading's best performances of the season.

Wimbledon

~ Playing Record ~

Competition	Played (Total)	Home					Away					Total	
		W	D	L	F	A	W	D	L	F	A	F	A
League	12	3	1	2	8	7	1	3	2	5	5	13	12

The adventures of Wimbledon F.C. are something of a fairy story finishing, some would say, in horror! A highly respected Amateur club of old, they turned professional, gained entry to the Football League, and on to the top division; won the F.A.Cup, lost their ground, and dropped to the lowest division, under the guise of 'Milton Keynes Dons'.

Over the years the two clubs have met infrequently, only in Friendly matches and a handful of League games. But the strangest coincidence occurred on the 14th of September 2002, when the ('new') Dons won 1-0 at The Madejski Stadium. On the same day, at non-League level, Reading Town (of the Combined Counties League), beat the 'other' Dons (the breakaway 'AFC Wimbledon')!

Three men that have been involved with both clubs include Les Henry, who had a seven-year playing record at Elm Park, and after two years in Ireland became The Dons manager. He stayed at Plough Lane for 17 years, and is seen as the main orchestrator of the club's rise to fame. Big money signing Keith Curle spent just a year at Elm Park before moving to the South London club for a record £350,000 fee, and Lawrie Sanchez, later a manager, joined the Dons after making over 300 appearances for Reading, and scored the only goal of the 1989 F.A.Cup Final.

Wisbech Town

The

Biscuitmen

Competition	Played	Home					Away					Total	
	(Total)	W	D	L	F	A	W	D	L	F	A	F	A
F.A.Cup	1	1	0	0	2	1	0	0	0	0	0	2	1

~ Playing Record ~

The 1957/58 season saw these two successful teams compete in the second round of the F.A.Cup. Reading, despite a shaky start, finished fifth in the Third Division South, just a few points off promotion, whilst their opponents, Wisbech Town from Cambridgeshire, finished as runners-up in the highly rated (part professional) Midland League.

Swindon had already been beaten by Reading in the first round, the, local derby attracting over 21,000, and even the second round with their non-League opponents produced an Elm Park gate of 17,000 plus. Wisbech had already shown themselves to be worthy opponents having already overcome (Third Division) Colchester United 1-0 at the same stage, before a near record attendance of 6,540 at Fenland Park. This had been the Fenmen's seventh game that season in the Cup!

However, the match went pretty well to form, despite the close final result, with the club's two leading goalscorers, centre-foreward Tommy Dixon, and his inside partner Jimmy Whitehouse each scoring to produce a 2-1 victory. Nothing remarkable in the game or the result, although the Elm Park fans were later praised in the local Cambridgeshire press for their friendly attitude by a visiting supporter.

The Cup run was shortlived that season, since the team lost in the third round to Leyton Orient.

Wolverhampton Wanderers

~ Playing Record ~

Competition	Played (Total)	Home					Away					Total	
		W	D	L	F	A	W	D	L	F	A	F	A
# League	28	7	3	4	25	15	4	2	8	15	23	40	38
* F.A.Cup													
League Cup	2	2	0	0	5	2	0	0	0	0	0	5	2

Matches with the Wolves have been fairly infrequent, with a gap of 54 years in league matches from 1935, and the 2002/03 season First Division play-off semi-final offers the most drama.

Having been promoted a year earlier from Division Two, the chance to move to the top division via the play-offs was offered. Wolverhampton Wanderers first stood in the way, with the first tie at Molineux which was not an easy hurdle. But rather than play for a draw, The Royals set about winning the game. They dominated the first half and were rewarded with a 25th minute goal from Nicky Forster. The game appeared to be heading Reading's way, before The Wolves sneaked in two late goals to take a 2-1 lead to the Madejski Stadium.

Despite this result, the second leg was looked upon with anticipation by the Reading fans, who felt they could turn the tie around. Not surprisingly the visitors were intent only on holding onto their lead, and once again The Royals dominated the game. As the minutes ticked by desperation began to set in, and then, cruelly, a breakaway by Wolves, settled the issue.

Despite the defeat, the club and fans could look back on a very rewarding season - and more were to come!

Workington

The

Biscuitmen

The Cumbrians time in the Football League (most of which was in the Fourth Division) was only from 1950 to 1977, therefore the meetings between the two clubs were limited to just six seasons.

The two met in the last game of the 1966/67 season, a match which was important for Reading. They were still in with a slight chance of promotion, needing to win the match at Borough Park. Courtesy of goals from Ron Foster, and top marksman George Harris - a free scoring winger who only missed one of the 51 matches played that season, The Biscuitmen duly achieved their objective, with a narrow 2-1 victory. But Middlesbrough clinched the second promotion spot (finishing with two more points), and Reading had to be content with fourth place, as Watford pipped them into third with a superior goal average. Until Watford equalised late in their match, and Middlesbrough (who won their last game in hand), the team were actually top of the table.

The attendance at Workington was a dreadful 856, with the homesters already doomed for relegation (they finished bottom). This was the first sub-thousand crowd that Reading had played before in the Football League, and a good proportion of those spectators were from Elm Park.

Wrexham

~ Playing Record ~

Competition	Played (Total)	Home					Away					Total	
		W	D	L	F	A	W	D	L	F	A	F	A
League	26	9	2	2	26	8	6	1	6	17	19	43	27
F.A.Cup	3	1	0	1	4	2	0	1	0	1	1	5	3

Alan Pardew's baptism in management, in October 1999, was far from ideal, with a traumatic first month, which included home defeats to Wigan and Oxford, and a 5-0 thumping at Millwall. At this time the club was staring relegation in the face, which made his appointment all the more a gamble.

The supporters felt that much of the team's problems were due to a distinct lack of effort on the part of the players, and the new manager who appeared to be unable to motivate them. For the match at home to Wrexham, just before Christmas, which followed on from a run of six matches without a victory, those fans decided to designate the occasion, as 'PANTS' day - the abbreviation of 'Players Are Not Trying Sufficiently'. Although not appreciated by the players themselves, many supporters - Chairman John Madejski included - proceeded to wave a large variety of underwear during the game.

The game itself was not a huge success, finishing as a 2-2 draw (draws perhaps being a feature of the day!), but meetings after the match between various factions had the desired effect. The club gradually rose in the Second Division table, to finish 10th, and of course Alan Pardew continued on to greater achievements.

Wycombe Wanderers

~ Playing Record ~

Competition	Played (Total)	Home					Away					Total	
		W	D	L	F	A	W	D	L	F	A	F	A
League	8	4	0	0	8	2	2	1	1	9	8	17	10
* F.A.Cup	1	0	0	0	0	0	1	0	0	2	1	2	1
League Cup	2	0	1	0	1	1	0	0	1	0	2	1	3

The Royals made a reasonably good start to the 2000/01 season (which was to eventually lead to promotion from Division Two), and played two impressive matches in the Worthington (League) Cup early in the season against Premiership clubs, beating West Ham (on penalties) and only narrowly losing to Aston Villa. On the 22nd of September, they entertained Wycombe Wanderers, a match which produced two 'milestones'.

The game, in which Reading dominated against a poor Wycombe side, was won 2-0. Adie Williams opened the scoring, a simple goal from close range after 16 minutes, and when Darius Henderson added a second two minutes later, this strike represented the 5,000th scored by Reading in the Football League. Henderson also went into the record books as being the first youngster to have progressed from the club's Youth Academy and on to play in the first team. The final scoreline was hardly a true reflection of the match, for it was only poor finishing that prevented The Royals from making it more comprehensive.

This was Williams' only goal of the season, despite playing in most games, and Henderson's first. He went on to score in the return match with Wycombe (which was also won 2-0), and made 38 League appearances that season.

Yeovil Town

The

Biscuitmen

~ *Playing Record* ~

Competition	Played (Total)	Home					Away					Total	
		W	D	L	F	A	W	D	L	F	A	F	A
F.A.Cup	1	1	0	0	4	2	0	0	0	0	0	4	2

The Somerset club made their name as giantkillers in the F.A.Cup, and did not become members of the Football League until 2003. By this time The Royals were playing in Division One (second level), and therefore the two have yet to meet in the League.

The pair first met in the 1946/47 season - technically not within the scope of this book since it was a Friendly match. Probably best forgotten by Reading supporters anyway, since the team was thrashed 5-0, in the oozing mud and the six-foot gradient (the notorious Huish pitch slope), as described by the local press.

The only competitive match, to date, was during the 1999/2000 season, in the F.A.Cup. By then Yeovil were a leading club in the Vauxhall Conference, and therefore were still not to be taken lightly. Entering in the round before, they beat Witney Town in the 4th qualifying round, which earned them a trip to the Madejski Stadium in November.

Reading eventually won the match comfortably by 4-2, but the non-League team were hardly outplayed, and fought back after Andy Bernal had given the homesters the lead after 30 minutes, to make the score 1-1 at the break. In the second period the Royals become more dominant, adding three goals to their tally, before Yeovil scored a late consolation second.

York City

The

Biscuitmen

~ Playing Record ~

Competition	Played	Home					Away					Total	
	(Total)	W	D	L	F	A	W	D	L	F	A	F	A
League	20	7	2	1	14	4	4	4	2	13	12	27	16
F.A.Cup	3	0	0	1	1	3	0	1	1	2	4	3	7

It is appropriate that the last alphabetical entry should also relate to a Reading victory. But unfortunately, the match in question was referred to as one of the worst games ever played at Elm Park!

The game in question was that of the 24th of October 1959. The Biscuitmen had made a dreadful start to the season, having lost seven of their first eight games, and by the late Autumn had only just begun to improve. The period in fact saw a home win by 6-3, and a very gratifying 4-0 thrashing of Swindon Town at the County Ground. Bouyant after such a comprehensive local derby victory, the team no doubt went into the York match full of confidence. The Minster team meanwhile struggled throughout the season, and only just avoided relegation.

Little space has been left to report on the game, since there was little of merit to comment on! Peter Shreeve scored the only goal, and the only real highlight came from Charlie Tissell. A bizarre shot from the York player was so badly hit that it struck the floodlights, and broke the glass covering, which showered a policeman sitting behind the goal!

The last League match played by the pair was a 1-1 draw in January 1999, at Bootham Crescent (currently known as Kit-Kat Crescent!)

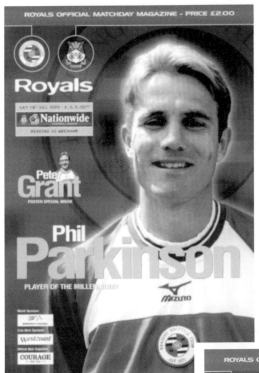

(Top) The programme for the PANTS day match versus Wrexham!

(Below, left) Williams, whose strike against Wycombe was Reading's 4,999th goal scored in The Football League.

(Below, right)
Never met in the Football League, this was the matchday programme for the Cup game versus Yeovil Town.

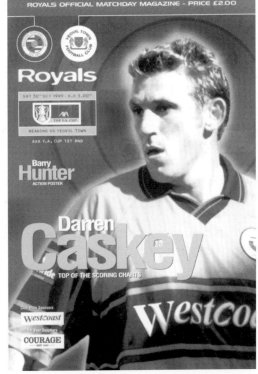

ACCRINGTON STANLEY

When Accrington Stanley (a completely separate club from the Football League founder-member club 'Accrington F.C.') resigned from the League in 1962, Oxford United were elected in their place; 44 years later, the two clubs effectively swapped places when United were relegated from the League and Stanley were the Football Conference Champions in the 2005/06 season and were promoted. An additional coincidence is that Accrington's last Football League team before they resigned included former Reading player Bill Smith and Oxford's final Football League game before their relegation include Matt Robinson in their line-up, a player they had signed from Reading.

ASTON VILLA

Reading and Aston Villa first met in the League in the 1970/71 season, and Reading players scored seven of the 11 goals in the two games; but they still lost both games! Reading players in fact scored three 'own goals, in that total. Terry Bell's own goal in effect relegated the club in the final game of the season which was played at Villa Park.

BLACKPOOL

Blackpool's 7-0 win over Reading in the 1930/31 season remains the Seaside club's highest victory in the League. Two of the goals were scored by John Oxberry who later played for Reading before becoming a coach at Elm Park.

BRISTOL CITY

On the 30th of March 2002, Reading led Bristol City by three goals to two after just 14 minutes.

BRISTOL ROVERS
Jamie Cureton became the first player to score a hat-trick at the Madejski Stadium during the 1998/99 season - but at this time he was a Bristol Rovers player. His four goals in total produced an embarrassing 6-0 defeat for The Royals, with all six coming in the second half. Three weeks after signing for Reading he then became the first Reading player to score a hat-trick at the ground, versus Brentford in September 2000.

BURNLEY
In the 2006/07 season, Reading's team that started in the third round FA Cup tie against Burnley, featured players either born in or capped for 11 different countries. The International players came from Cameroon, Ecuador, Iceland, Nigeria, South Korea, U.S.A. and Wales, with the remaining players having been born in Australia the Democratic Republic of the Congo and Ireland. This left just one Englishman in the line-up, who was named Scott!

CRYSTAL PALACE
1961/62 was the first season when the Football League allowed member clubs to play pre-season Friendlies matches against other League clubs (previously 'inhouse' - 'Possibles v Probables' type encounters had to suffice). Reading's first such Friendly was a 7-2 victory over Crystal Palace.

DONCASTER ROVERS
The three managers appointed by this club between 1994 and 1997, were all former Reading players: Sammy Chung, from the 1950's, was replaced by Kerry Dixon, before David Cowling took over. Cowling had only been a Reading player for five months, but his time in the hot seat at Doncaster, lasted just 10 days!

EXETER CITY
Reading first issued matchday programmes in the 1880's, but on the 26th of October 1947, versus Exeter City, that edition was designated 'Volume 1 Number 1', and this sequence has continued. The programme was initially known as 'The Elm Park Journal', when it contained eight pages and cost 2d (1.5p).

HARTLEPOOL UNITED
Reading's trainer, Jimmy Wallbanks, came on to the pitch to treat an injured player when The Royals first visited the Victoria Ground in September 1973. But he entered the playing area without the permission of the Referee and was consequently 'booked'. Therefore, just a few days short of his 64th Birthday, Jimmy became the oldest person to be booked in a League game.

MANCHESTER UNITED
Reading's first Premiership encounters against United, produced four club records:

1 The match at the Madejski Stadium saw Manchester United become the 100th club to play Reading in the Football League.

2 The return encounter at Old Trafford was seen by 75,910, the highest ever to watch a game involving Reading.

3 The fifth round FA Cup tie at Old Trafford, was the first Reading game to be shown in full on live terrestrial television.

4 The F.A.Cup replay saw United 3-0 ahead after 5 minutes and 41 seconds – the fastest three goal lead in British senior football (Reading's comeback gave a final result of 3-2).

MIDDLESBROUGH
Prior to the 2006-07 Premiership season, the six previous seasons in which the two clubs played in the same division, Middlesbrough were promoted at the end of each.

NEWPORT COUNTY
Newport's 2-1 win over Reading in the League Cup on 19 August 1970 was somewhat of a surprise result since Reading were in a division higher than County. This transpired to be Newport's only win until the middle of January 1971, a run of 28 games that produced 23 defeats and four draws.

PLYMOUTH ARGYLE
Frank Richardson was the first Argyle player to score four times in a League game, and he later became the first Reading player to achieve that total. The quartet of goals helped Reading win the Third Division South championship in the final game of 1925/26 when Brentford were beaten, for they secured the one promotion place, edging Plymouth into second.

PORTSMOUTH
Reading were the first team to play a Southern League game at Fratton Park, the visitors losing 2-0 on 9 September 1899 before a crowd of 9,000.

PORT VALE
Then known as 'Burslem Port Vale', the Potteries club became the first professional team to play Reading when they visited the club's old Caversham Cricket Ground on 27 December 1892. Despite missing several first team players, including captain Frank Deane (who decided to go ice skating instead!), Reading won 2-1 and the match produced (then) record gate receipts of £24-5-6d.

QUEEN'S PARK RANGERS
QPR were the visitors for Reading's final home game of 2005/06 and for the first time since they had moved to the Madejski Stadium, The Royals' season ended with a match that had no effect on either promotion or relegation. Despite the game being in effect meaningless, 23,156 celebrating fans attended, when they witnessed Reading break the Football League record with 106 points.

SHREWSBURY TOWN
Graham French was just 16 years 177 days old when he made his debut for Shrewsbury against Reading in September 1961 and he remains The Shrews' youngest ever League player. In 1973, he appeared for Reading in three matches whilst on loan from Luton Town.

SOUTHAMPTON
The first F.A.Cup-tie ever staged in Hampshire, took place on the Antelope Ground on 24 October 1891 when Southampton played host to Reading. Despite Southampton winning 7-0, Reading went on to the next round, for the result was declared void, Southampton being disqualified for fielding ineligible players.

TOTTENHAM HOTSPUR
When Reading played Tottenham on 13 February 2007 they fielded four of their five most expensive players; this starting eleven being the costliest the club had ever fielded. Yet remarkably the £5.5 million of Reading talent was playing in a reserve fixture.

WIGAN ATHLETIC
When Wigan travelled to Elm Park on 2 November 1985 the referee decided that their all white shirts clashed with Reading's blue and white strip, so the visitors had to wear Reading's yellow away kit. Coincidentally, seven years later, Reading were required to wear Wigan's away kit at Springfield Park when the two clubs colours again clashed.

The end of a
'Journey',
that started in 1920,
at the Elm Park Ground...

and the (old) Third Division....

and finishes (or more accurately)
pauses....

In 2007 in The Premiership...

At the Madejski Stadium

Yore Publications

(Established 1991 by Dave Twydell)

We specialise in football books (only), normally with an historic theme.

Especially: Comprehensive Football League club histories, over 30 to date,
notably: 'Heaven On Earth' (The Official History of Reading F.C.),
plus Bolton Wanderers, Partick Thistle, Rochdale, Hull City, etc.

Also players 'Who's Who' books, recent clubs include:
Oldham Athletic, Brentford, Queens Park Rangers, Notts. County etc.

Other titles of a more unusual nature include:
'The Ultimate Directory of English and Scottish Football League Grounds"
(An encyclopaedia detailing every ground on which a League match has been played)
'Through The Turnstiles Again' (A history of football related to attendances)
'Rejected F.C.' (A series of books providing the histories of former Football League clubs.

Plus non-League - The 'Gone But Not Forgotten' series
(histories of defunct non-League clubs and former grounds)

Yore Publications, 12 The Furrows, Harefield, Middx. UB9 6AT
~ See our Website: www.yore.demon.co.uk which includes all our current titles ~
Or: Send a s.a.e. for a copy of our latest Newsletter